NORMAN
'BLACK JAKE'
UPRICHARD

NORMAN 'BLACK JAKE' UPRICHARD

with CHRIS WESTCOTT

AMBERLEY

First published 2011

Amberley Publishing
The Hill, Stroud
Gloucestershire, GL5 4EP

www.amberleybooks.com

British Library Cataloguing in Publication Data.
A catalogue record for this book is available from the British Library.

ISBN 978-1-4456-0088-8

Typesetting and Origination by Amberley Publishing.
Printed in Great Britain.

Contents

Foreword by Harry Gregg

I am delighted to add my name to this tribute to Norman, who was an unbelievable character. He was known as 'Black Jake' because he managed to get a lift to an international match on the back of a coal lorry – he turned up covered in coal dust! Norman was older than I am and was the Irish goalkeeper before me. I came into the international side in 1954; we beat England at Wembley for the first time in 1957, and went on to the 1958 World Cup finals in Sweden. During that time, and through our lives, Norman and I always remained great friends.

Norman wasn't a big man for a keeper. Peter Doherty's expression was that anybody could play in an empty room, but there was no empty room for goalkeepers in those days. You were under pressure no matter what. Norman played in an era when football, as well as being a wonderful, exciting game, was physical as well. You had to compete and sometimes you got hurt, which happened to Norman on many occasions. When I watch goalkeepers nowadays they never catch a ball, they palm every ball out and then they pick it up. In our day, even in training, if you palmed the ball they would tell you to catch it. You daren't palm a ball down, as you would have no fingers left trying to pick it up. Norman was a brave keeper. He went to Arsenal as a youngster, but his best time was at Portsmouth.

In the World Cup Finals we were allowed twenty-three players in a pool, but we only had seventeen, because the selectors felt we didn't have enough quality in depth, so we went short-handed. There might have been one or two in that group who felt that they were better than the rest, but generally there was a very good spirit within the players. We were the first team to knock previous world champions, Italy, out of the World Cup and it was part of a wonderful time for Norman and me as players.

Our trainer, Gerry Morgan, was a marvellous man. Today the game has changed dramatically, with psychiatrists and all sorts of people involved, many having nothing to do with football. Gerry was the first psychiatrist, or psychologist, for want of a better expression; he kept everybody happy. He was a most wonderful old character to have around the camp. Everybody loved Gerry. He relieved the pressure from us.

There was a deadline for everybody to be in at our World Cup headquarters at Halmstad in Sweden. It was a beautiful place and we were sitting around late one evening when Peter Doherty said to Gerry, 'Everybody in?' and Gerry said, 'Yes, Peter, everybody's in.' With that you could hear a whistle coming from this lovely path through the woods and it was Norman whistling 'The Sash My Father Wore' (which is a tribal ballad here in Ireland), and playing with coins in his pocket as if he was playing the drums. Peter said, 'Gerry I thought you said they were all in. Norman where have you been?' Norman said, 'I'm not the only bloody one out, McIlroy's down there with a bird!' We got to our room that night and Gerry, this huge old man, was lying in bed across from me saying, 'He was a bloody stool pigeon, I wouldn't let anybody down.' That was the character he was.

I wish this publication every success; it is certainly a story worth telling.

Chapter One

The First of Many...

If medicals were as thorough in the 1940s as they are now, I would never have been a professional footballer, never won eighteen full international caps and never played over 300 games as a professional footballer. Let me explain.

As a twelve-year-old my pals and I were always climbing, and one day I fell off a wall that was about 12 feet high, onto a Guinness bottle. It went right through my right hand; I still have the scar. I ran into the house with the bottle still impaled in my hand and my mother promptly fainted! A neighbour four doors down, a Mrs McCusker, put my hand in a basin of water and called the doctor, who stopped the bleeding. The next day I had to go down to the children's hospital at the Falls Road in Belfast. The doctor said I had two options, to leave the hand as it was and I would gradually get the flexibility back, or he could join the sinews together, but my hand would be permanently stiff. I took the first option.

To be quite honest, I don't know how I ever played football and had the career I had with my hand like that. With the medicals the way they are now I would never have passed, as one finger in particular was never right. It was the first of many injuries I suffered in my life, albeit the others were on the football field. However, I loved football so much I would go through all the pain again. Fate, or chance, plays a huge part in the lives of us all, and goalkeeping injuries regularly featured in the development of my career in football.

I was born William Norman McCourt in the town of Moyraverty between Lurgan and Portadown, Northern Ireland, on 20 April 1928 and shared the same birthday as Hitler! I was the only child of hard-working parents. My mother, Henrietta, worked at McCalls' Linen Mill, as the area had been a major centre for the production of textiles since the Industrial Revolution. My father, Stephen, worked in Wells' Quarry but sadly died after a long illness when I was only six. He had tuberculosis for sixteen weeks before he passed away. During that time my mother had to take me to school, and pick me up, on the saddle of her bike.

My father Stephen.

Dr Deaney gave my father a medicine called Robeline in a carton. When he became too ill to take it, my mother gave it to me, together with fried eggs, fried bread and spuds, which was our diet. It never did me any harm. The first time I saw meat I didn't know what it was, as we lived off the land with potatoes and vegetables. When the bread man came round once a week we bought a couple of loaves and made potato bread with it on the open fire. We cut it into four and fried it; it was lovely stuff, like soda bread. After my father died it took my mother three years' wages to pay off the doctor's bill.

Before my father passed away he instilled in me an interest in football. We played with a tennis ball outside the house all the time. Although neither he, nor any of his relatives, ever seriously played football, he was a dedicated supporter of Glenavon Football Club. He never missed a game, home or away, and thought little of cycling up to Ballymena, Coleraine or Derry, whatever the weather. It was probably that enthusiasm that led to his death at the age of twenty-seven, as sometimes he got drenched on his bike on the long trail back from an away match. He started taking me on the bar of his bike every Saturday to watch them at home when I was about four years old.

Father holding me as a wee boy.

After my father died, my uncles bought me a bike between the four of them. It wasn't new, but they made it up for me. I was able to cycle into town and paid a penny to get in through the turnstile. I always stood in the same place as my father. I left the bike unchained – it was never a problem in those days, it would be there next week. My uncles would bring the *Ireland's Saturday Night*, known as 'The Ulster', round to our country cottage as it reported on all the games. My favourite teams were Arsenal, Glasgow Rangers, and Belfast Celtic. I read the paper on Sunday mornings to see how Arsenal got on, never thinking one day I would play for them, or scout a season for Rangers.

Among my heroes at the time in the Glenavon side were big Joe Clayton, centre-half and policeman; left back Mick Hoy, who came from Sugar Island close to where we lived; outside right Freddie Holbeach, who came from Wolves; Jack Jones, who was right half; and Chappie Craig, who hailed from around Donacloney, and was centre forward.

Later I got to know Hugh Kelly, the great Glenavon goalkeeper, who moved to Belfast Celtic, then across to England to play for Fulham, Southampton and Exeter. He was a local lad, who made good and played four times for Ireland;

I wished I could play like that. I also remember that Walter Rickett, who I came across later in my career, was playing for Ballymena at the time, against Glenavon.

My mother and I were left in a poor way when my father died. We lived in an isolated little house and often I didn't have any boots, let alone a pair of football boots. But my mother always made sure I had plenty of grub. I used to cut four lengths of sticks from bushes to make my own goalposts. Pieces of rope provided the crossbars and I always had a ball of sorts and never tired of dribbling from one set of goals to the other, beating hundreds of imaginary defenders on the way. I had to do it all on my own in those childhood days because we lived in such a remote place. If it was raining I played in the parlour of our house. We kept the hay for the cow there, and I liked to throw a tennis ball against the wall and dive into the hay to catch it. It was early goalkeeping practice, although I didn't realise it at the time.

Soon after my father died we moved to Albert Street in Lurgan, County Armagh, near the southern shore of Lough Neagh. I started at the Model School on the outskirts of town, which was a mixed school. As a wee boy of six, starting school with no father was tough; my mother had to work nine hours a day to get a living. I used to have a very bad stammer, as I sat beside a little fella called Kevin Toman; he stuttered and, sitting beside him, I got into the habit. There was a time when if somebody asked me my name I couldn't say it because of my stammer, so I had to write it down; I felt so embarrassed. When we moved to Lurgan from the countryside I was frightened of policemen, ministers and priests – not that I'd done anything wrong. I would shake when I saw them, and the nerves made my stammer worse. However, when I started playing football in the wide open spaces of Lurgan, I gradually became more confident and grew out of it. I have no problems now – try and stop me talking – but for sport, I may still have had the stammer.

During the Second World War, I was nicknamed 'u-boat' as my name began with 'U'. That disappeared once I finished at school.

It was there that I first played competitive football and eventually made the school team. Because of the war the schools' league had ceased to operate, but we played friendly games against schools like Kingspark and Carrick. The Lunn brothers, Harry and Bertie, who later played for Glenavon, Notts County, Swindon Town and Bournemouth, played for Carrick School then. I would catch up with Harry during my career. To my mind he was one of the best right wingers to come out of Ireland, but couldn't get into the international team because of Billy Bingham.

The two best players in our side were Denny Denver, who later played for Glenavon and Belfast Celtic, and Bill Dickson, who played twelve games for

Northern Ireland and was the finest centre half I ever played behind in my professional career. When you called for the ball he'd give it to you; he didn't do any fancy stuff and was a very safe player. In the short time I played with him he impressed me hugely, he was actually an inside forward but a very versatile player. Bill started at Glenavon, then joined Notts County in 1945 and moved to Chelsea as part of the Tommy Lawton deal in 1947. Tom Whitaker paid £15,000 for him to join Arsenal in 1953 but he was very unlucky with injuries. He slipped a disc twice, dislocated a shoulder, injured his knee, broke his wrist and also suffered a triple fracture of his nose in an FA Cup semi-final. But, apart from that, he had a good run, free of injury! Bill returned to Glenavon in 1958.

Lurgan, with a population of something like 14,000, had produced more international players than any other town in Ireland. Others included the brothers Jack and Sam Jones and their brother-in-law Billy Mitchell. Jack went to Scotland and played for Hibs, Sam went across to Blackpool, and Billy also crossed the water to Chelsea. In fact, they all played in the half-back line for Ireland against Scotland at Edinburgh in 1936. George Moorhead was another Lurgan boy who played four times for Northern Ireland in the 1920s, and Walter 'Paddy' Sloane was another international who played for fifteen clubs and was the first Irishman to play in Italian Serie 'A' football. Tragically, his brother fell off a ladder putting up a Christmas tree in the town centre. Then there was Jimmy Magill and Neil Lennon. Quite why there were so many I don't know, but there were some very good footballers around when I was at school.

I began as an outside right before fate played a 'hand'. One Saturday I had a bit of a cold, so my mother told me I was not to play football until I felt better. We had a game against a school from Moira which I went along to watch at Lurgan Park complete with overcoat, scarf and balaclava. When I arrived we had no goalkeeper, so the schoolmaster asked me to deputise for him. I explained about my cold and he said, 'Go ahead, it will keep you warm.' We won the game 2 – 0 and I saved two penalties. The master actually already realised I had some goalkeeping ability, as he used to put me between two sticks and kick at me with any sort of old ball, sometimes even a rag stuffed with hay and tied together. I didn't realise what he was doing at the time, but I became the regular goalkeeper for the Model School from that day onwards.

I took various balls with me to bed every night, and remember saving up four guineas to buy a pair of football boots which were called Hotspurs. They were my pride and joy: thick leather boots with a hard toe cap; I had to soak them in water to give them a bit of flexibility.

Chapter Two

Banned for Life

Until 1971, rule twenty-seven of the Gaelic Athletic Association constitution stated that a member of the GAA could be banned from participating in its games if found also to be playing soccer, rugby or cricket. As a youngster, of course, all I ever wanted to do was play sport.

I must have been a nipper of about thirteen when we moved from Albert Street to Wellington Street, still in Lurgan. I was a Protestant and most of the people in the street were Catholic. All my mates lived in the North Street district of Lurgan.

It was there that I first came into contact with Bobby Carville, who was the 'Demon Barber of Wellington Street' for nearly fifty years. Bobby was always keen on sport and there was nothing about sport he didn't know. In his barber's he had a cupboard full of sports books. Anything you wanted to know, he had a book on it. He would be cutting your hair and, if somebody asked him a question about sport, he would leave you halfway through your haircut and look up the answer in one of his books! After a couple of haircuts he would rush outside to kick a tennis ball at me. He put me in goal between a wall and a telegraph pole. He was a marvellous character, and organised street teams into a league in which I played for Wellington Rovers.

In about 1943 Bobby asked me if I wanted to play for St Peter's Gaelic Football minor team, which he started up and managed. I said I couldn't as they played on a Sunday and I was supposed to go to Sunday school in the afternoon and would be wearing all my best clothes. Also, of course, I was a Protestant. He said it didn't matter, as at the time there was no organised schools football and I wasn't playing association football. I could walk up Church Walk and come back down North Street, and nobody would see me. Because of my love of sport I thought more of playing football than going to Sunday school and my mother, fortunately, didn't find out for years.

I was away playing goalie at places such as Derrymacash. One game in particular stands out in my mind against Tiranog, who came from the 'tunnel'

Wellington St 1930s

Bobby Carville, the 'Demon Barber of Wellington Street'.

in Portadown. We needed two points to win the League and ran out winners 13 – 12. As the game finished the crowd rushed the field and we had to flee for our lives as they set upon us in no uncertain manner. The old girls came out with their hurley sticks and chased us up the street – Tiranog were favourites and they didn't like their team losing. Danny Bailey, who wasn't a 'full shilling', got split on the head with a stick and we had to run for about three miles for the train. I finished up changing at Portadown Railway Station and discovered, to my horror, I had two odd shoes. That Sunday night I sat at home with one foot over the other for fear my mother might see it, as of course she thought I had been to church. I got it sorted out the following day with Oliver Healey, one of our team. In the rush to avoid the trouble after the game he had put on one of my shoes. If my mother had found out, she would have probably beaten the hell out of me, but in later years she didn't hold it against me. My father was a staunch Orange man; of course I would never have dared play Gaelic football in the first place if he was alive.

I played thirteen out of fourteen games that 1943–44 season and we won the Lurgan and Portadown District League. I'd just turned sixteen when, shortly after, Glenavon approached me. I was kicking around with some of the boys on a little patch of open ground opposite to where we lived and Andy Wiley, the

Glenavon manager was watching. There was no Irish League during the war, but the Juniors had started up and he asked me to play in goal in the Mid-Ulster League. Bobby Carville said it would be a good move, and Andy signed me.

Then the GAA got to know about me signing for Glenavon and I received a letter from them suspending me from all Gaelic participation *sine die*. I expected the ban, as you weren't allowed to play both games – it was Protestant against Catholic. It was an unjust rule to my thinking because you should be able to play whatever sport you want to. The local Textile Hall was about fifty yards from where we lived and on the night St Peter's had their dance and presentation of medals, I could hear the music from our front door. It was the first time I had ever won anything and because of the ban I wasn't invited, so I wandered up there at about 8.30 a.m. I saw everybody enjoying themselves and I walked back home, went straight upstairs to bed and cried my eyes out.

In 2003, I was invited over to Ireland for the weekend, with the survivors of the 1958 World Cup squad and we stayed at the Silverwood Hotel in Lurgan. The owner, Sean Hughes, mentioned in passing that he was on the committee of St Peter's Gaelic Football Association. I said I played for them all those years ago but never received a medal, being suspended for being involved in a foreign game (soccer). Some months later in January 2004 I received an invite from Sean to the club's annual dinner, where I was guest of honour. To my surprise and amazement I was presented with the medal, plus a beautiful framed photograph of myself diving at the feet of the great Tommy Lawton at Highbury. It brought tears to my eyes and was one of the few times in my life that I've been completely lost for words. It was heart rendering and an incredibly emotional evening that cut across all religions. So I finally received my medal, forty-four years later!

It was a fantastic gesture by the club, and put things right. I believe that was the stepping stone to my playing career, because if I had not started playing with St Peter's, whether it be soccer or Gaelic, I might not have played at all for any team. However, I enjoyed my season playing goalie and it didn't do my goalkeeping any harm. I never forget the people of Wellington Street and North Street for their hospitality and kindness every time I go back over there. My appreciation of them dates all the way back to when they presented me with a radio at a Bangor Hotel after I won my first senior cap. On the same occasion, Alfie McMichael, on behalf of all the players, presented the incomparable Peter Doherty with a box of linen. I think the world of the folk of Lurgan; their kindness and hospitality is always overwhelming.

I call Lurgan 'home' and Maurice Magee always has a car at the airport for me whenever I return there. I'd also like to mention another couple of friends, Oliver Burns, a local historian, who has always kept in touch with me, and Maurice O'Reilly, who also played for St Peter's, albeit after me.

St Peter's 2004 annual dinner, when I finally received my Gaelic football medal. Pictured with friends Maurice Magee and Maurice O'Reilly.

Framed photo of Tommy Lawton presented at the dinner. From left: Paul McGrane, myself, John McStravick, Joe McDonald and Benedict Lavery.

Glenavon was a pretty inexperienced side that first season (1944–45), playing against teams like Armagh Whites. I had plenty to do and, although I had to pick more balls out of the net than I care to remember, I did gain valuable experience. The following year (1945–46), the reserves entered the Intermediate League and we managed to finish in the top half of the table. I had such a decent season that Albert Mitchell, who ran Lisburn Distillery Seconds and scouted for Portsmouth, invited me to move to Distillery Football Club, who were playing in the Belfast Regional League. I was also playing in the Portadown Summer League for a team called Aston Villa, and after one of their matches a guy called Billy Bradley asked me if I would sign for Belfast Celtic. I couldn't get the pen quick enough, but I never heard another word from them and Distillery got me to cancel the Celtic signing.

Off the pitch, I left school when I was fourteen and started to work as an apprentice textile fitter for a firm called Carson and Robertson, who had a factory in the Ligoniel district of Belfast. It was a journey of twenty miles each way, every day, and I travelled up and down on the workman's train, which left Lurgan at 6.45 a.m. each morning. As a first year apprentice I was earning fifteen shillings (75p) per week, which was a pittance. After paying the train fare my residual income was very small. However, the Distillery Club agreed to pay my weekly fare and travel expenses for matches wherever they were, which was one of the reasons I agreed to join them.

Then, part of the factory moved nearer home to Lisburn, only about twelve miles away from Lurgan, which suited me. I've always been a bit of a rebel, which has got me into trouble from time to time, and we had machines to put on top of the looms to weave patterns. When I was a second year apprentice, there was a consignment going out one day and a spring on one of the machines was a bit loose. The boss, Mr Carson, said to me, 'Hi boy.' I replied politely, 'Yes Mr Carson.' 'Lend me your chisel,' he said. I went to my drawer and it wasn't there. I said to Carson, 'Sorry Mr Carson, somebody must have borrowed it.' 'What kind of a fitter are you? Go to Ligoniel in the morning,' he shouted. I said, 'Mr Carson, you go and f—k yourself!' I got my coat and walked out – it wasn't my fault my chisel wasn't there, someone must have borrowed it without telling me, but he didn't see it like that.

That was on a Thursday. In the evening I went training at Distillery and told the reserve team trainer Dick Meek, a very nice man, what had happened. He phoned Jimmy McIlroy (not the footballer), who was the head man of Mather & Platt, a large engineering (sprinkler) firm from Manchester. He arranged a meeting with Mr McIlroy on the Friday morning at Bedford Street in Belfast. Whereas I was earning £2 and 7 shillings a week at Carson and Robertson, Mr McIlroy offered me £4 and 18 shillings a week with a bonus as an improver – which was a fitter of sorts, if jobs were completed within the timescale.

Distillery II, Intermediate Cup Winners 1947–48.

We jobbed all around Belfast at various mills and factories that could be vulnerable to fire. Charlie Tully and Jimmy Jones of Belfast Celtic were working there. Jimmy took me to work on the back of his motorbike; he was keen on bikes and took part in the North West 200 race. Jimmy and I were working up the Falls Road one day, putting sprinklers into Isaac Andrews Flour Mill when Jimmy forgot to put the little sprinkler in and the place was flooded! We were on our way home twenty miles away and didn't know anything about it. There was a hell of a rumpus about that and we received a right bollocking over it but never got the sack. People said to me for a long time after, 'Have you turned any sprinklers on lately Norman?'

When I joined Distillery they gave me a £25 signing on fee and my wages were £2 10 shillings a week, making over £6 a week, so I was doing quite well for myself and able to support my mother as well. At the time, the established first team goalkeeper was Billy Smyth, who played four times for Northern Ireland. So, during my two seasons with Distillery I played mainly for the second eleven,

A trademark dive at the feet of a forward during the Cup Final replay against Brantwood, which Distillery II won 5 – 4.

but I did gain a lot of experience with them. Before the end of the first season I was chosen to play in the Northern Ireland Juniors team that defeated Southern Ireland Juniors 4 – 0 on my home ground at Grosvenor Park. My senior debut was on 6 March 1947 in a 3 – 1 Regional League victory at Coleraine.

During the 1947–48 season the Distillery second team began to blend well in the Intermediate League. Whilst we finished mid-table, we did win the Intermediate Cup, defeating Brantwood 5 – 4 at the second attempt in the final, after a 1 – 1 draw. Many of my team mates would become regulars in the senior side – Sammy Dodds, John McClinton, Currie Mulholland, Maurice McVeigh, Rab Wilson, Jim Wilson and Bobby McLaughlin. I remember Tommy Dickson (later to become known by Linfield supporters at Windsor Park as the 'Duke of Windsor') was in the Brantwood team and showed every sign of the promise he later fulfilled, a very fine footballer.

My personal highlight of the season was being chosen to play for Northern Ireland Juniors against Scotland, at Cliftonville. We won 3 – 0 with goals from the Ballymoney trio of Taylor, Crowther and McAlea and, although he didn't score, our centre forward that day was Sammy Hughes of Glentoran, later to become a legend in his own right.

Repelling a Scottish attack in the 3 – 0 victory. Even at this early stage I'm wearing a bandage on my knee – a sign of further injuries to come.

Irish Junior International team that defeated Scotland 3 – 0 at Cliftonville, Belfast, in the 1947–48 season.

Irish Intermediate
League team,
which was
defeated 4 – 2
by the Scottish
Central League
at Firhill Park,
Glasgow, in
March 1948.

I also played in March 1948 for the Irish Intermediate League against the Scottish Central League in front of 11,000 at Firhill Park, Glasgow, where a host of scouts were present. Whilst we lost 4 – 2, Blackpool, Burnley, Huddersfield and Bury had, according to press reports, all been watching me, but Distillery placed a transfer fee of £3,000 on me, which, for a reserve team player, understandably put them off. The team that day was Uprichard, Barnes (Cliftonville Olympic), J. Barr (Linfield Swifts), Malone (Brantwood), Todd (Brantwood), McCarroll (Larne), Dubois (Linfield Swifts), Mulholland (Distillery), Hughes (Larne), Clarke (Crusaders), and Smyth (Ballyclare Comrades). The referee was Tom Wharton, who later became a leading FIFA referee.

It was a memorable season for me, even though I was kept out of the first eleven because of the consistent brilliance of Billy Smyth. I greatly admired Billy, who was a gentleman, as I also did Tommy Breen and Hugh Kelly of Belfast Celtic. However, since childhood my own personal hero had been Jerry Dawson of Glasgow Rangers. He was a brave and skilful keeper and I suppose I always wanted to emulate him.

Later in my career it was said that Bert Williams, the Wolves and England keeper was someone I wanted to aspire to. That's not quite correct. I didn't model myself on anyone but Bert, who was not the tallest but very agile, which I also needed to be, as I was only 5 foot 9 inches.

With two of my Distillery teammates Sammy Dodds and John McClinton, we were known as the 'Terrible Trio of Distillery', as once we collected our pay packet from the club, we'd go out on the town and have a few drinks. John was a bit of a comedian. He'd walk along Royal Avenue and suddenly shout, 'Look Norman, look Sammy, there's a monkey up there.' Before you knew there were a hundred people in the street gathered round looking up for a fictitious monkey! Boozy mates but innocent fun.

My first contact with English football was Charlton Athletic, who were touring Ireland and played Distillery in a friendly. After I finished work that day at Mather & Platt, I wanted to see Charlton play so went to Grosvenor Park only for the manager/secretary, Alf Peachey, to call me in to play as Billy Smyth wasn't well. After a hard day's work I was thrown in at the deep end – which wasn't ideal preparation. We lost 3 – 0, but I had a pretty good game. Afterwards Sam Bartram, the Charlton goalie, ran half the length of the field to shake my hand and said, 'Norman, you'll make it.' I never thought when he shook my hands and wished me all the best that I would be playing against him for Portsmouth years later. We became very good friends and I believe he was the finest keeper never to be capped for England.

Towards the end of the season the first eleven met Belfast Celtic at Celtic Park in the second round of the County Antrim Shield. I again went along to watch, only to learn on arrival that Billy had suddenly gone down with flu and I was playing. In the Celtic forward line that evening were Paddy Bonnar, Jimmy Jones and Charlie Tully. As a young lad, I was shaking – they were household names and I picked the ball out of the net four times, two each from Bonnar and Tully. It was the fifth time that season that Celtic had beaten Distillery, but I didn't disgrace myself. One report stated, 'The League champions were not flattered by the 4 – 0 score which might easily have been doubled but for the vigilance of Uprichard.' Our plans were disrupted by an injury to Eddie Lonsdale, a very fine defender, after just fifteen minutes. He courageously spent most of the game hobbling along the right wing and we sorely missed his steadying influence and experience. Eddie was a legend at the club, playing over 400 games in several positions including goal.

I suppose I must have had a reasonable game and fate would have it that, unknown to me, Arsenal officials had come to watch Billy. In his absence the Celtic forwards gave me plenty of opportunity to demonstrate what I could do. Arsenal's chief scout in Northern Ireland for ten years had been Joe McCleery and their manager, Tom Whittaker, who had never seen me play, greatly respected his judgement. On Joe's strong recommendation Arsenal were prepared to pay the transfer fee, which according to press reports, had been lowered to £1,500, even though I had only eleven senior appearances to my name. Distillery were happy to cash in on me in view of Billy's consistency and Alf Peachey agreed the terms, which included a further £500 if I played six games for the Arsenal first team.

Chapter Three

The Bright Lights of London

Tom Whittaker had been associated with Arsenal since 1919 and became manager of the famous club in 1947 on George Allison's retirement. In his first season, Arsenal won the League and I soon discovered that Tom was a great man and someone I developed the utmost respect for.

Tom, and Jack Crayston, his assistant, came over to Belfast and I signed for the Arsenal at the age of twenty on 3 June 1948. About a month later I arrived at Highbury in search of fame and fortune. Tom invited my mother and new girlfriend, Elizabeth, over at Arsenal's expense to make sure I was settled all right and we really enjoyed the week we had in London. It helped me settle in at the club, as I was initially completely overawed when I looked at the marble halls and bust of Herbert Chapman. It was unbelievable. What a transformation it was, from playing second team football in Ireland to being transferred to one of the most famous clubs in England. I was very well treated there and was able to stop my apprenticeship at Mather & Platt, as I hated the job and once I was at Arsenal I didn't need the extra wages. It knew more about me than I did about the fitting! My first wage at the Arsenal was £8 and 10 shillings a week and £6 and 10 shillings in the summer, which in those days wasn't bad at all. At Christmas time I became eligible for a thirty bob rise to £10 a week and it rose yearly in line with the FA wage structure.

However, my first impressions were a little disheartening, as Arsenal already had four highly competent goalkeepers, George Swindon, Ted Platt, George Dunkley and Jack Kelsey. A newspaper report at the time gave an assessment of the goalkeeping situation at Highbury:

George Swindon, although thirty-five years old, seems good at least for the coming campaign. His deputy is Ted Platt, quite a good goalkeeper, but far too liable to make elementary blunders. Arsenal's obvious successor is Norman Uprichard. Only twenty years old, this cat-like keeper seems certain of many international caps in the future.

Tom Whittaker (seated), the Arsenal manager, who I had huge respect for.

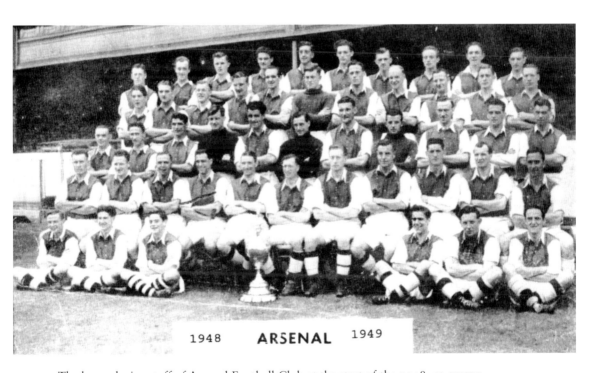

1948   **ARSENAL**   1949

The huge playing staff of Arsenal Football Club at the start of the 1948–49 season.

The goalkeeping complement at Arsenal in 1948 from left: Jack Kelsey, myself, George Swindon, Ted Platt and George Dunkley.

George was a brave keeper who dominated his penalty area and in his prime was second only to Frank Swift, England's number one. However, I was obviously hopeful of breaking through at some stage into the first team. Some doubted I would make a top-class keeper in view of my lack of height for a goalie, but there had been many sub-6-foot keepers in the past; Harry Hibbs didn't do too badly for example.

My first game at Highbury was a pre-season friendly on 7 August 1948, when the reserves played the first team. I think they beat us by six or seven goals, but it was a great experience, playing against the likes of Joe Mercer, Archie Macauley and Jimmy Logie. Jack Kelsey and I played alternate Saturdays in the third team. On my free Saturdays I usually watched the first team play but occasionally saw other London teams, including Spurs and Chelsea. It helped me see how First Division keepers did their job.

ARSENAL FOOTBALL CLUB, LTD.,
ARSENAL STADIUM, HIGHBURY, N.5.

PRICE ONE PENNY   **OFFICIAL PROGRAMME**   PRACTICE MATCH

Saturday, August 7th, 1948.   Kick off 3.15 p.m.

REDS (o)   WHITES (o)

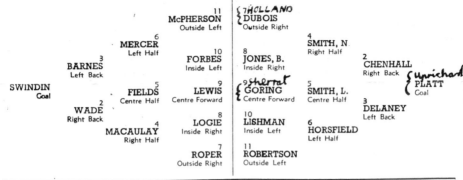

11
McPHERSON
Outside Left

7 HOLLAND
DUBOIS
Outside Right

6
MERCER
Left Half

4
SMITH, N.
Right Half

3
BARNES
Left Back

10
FORBES
Inside Left

8
JONES, B.
Inside Right

2
CHENHALL
Right Back

Uprichard
PLATT
Goal

SWINDIN
Goal

5
FIELDS
Centre Half

9
LEWIS
Centre Forward

9 Sherrat
GORING
Centre Forward

5
SMITH, L.
Centre Half

2
WADE
Right Back

8
LOGIE
Inside Right

10
LISHMAN
Inside Left

3
DELANEY
Left Back

4
MACAULAY
Right Half

6
HORSFIELD
Left Half

7
ROPER
Outside Right

11
ROBERTSON
Outside Left

Changes **will** be made at Half-Time, and details will be announced on the Loud Speaker.

Referee :—
Mr. R. C. GREENWOOD
(Norwood)

Linesmen :—
Mr. P. STRINGER (Abbey Wood)
White & Blue Flag.
Mr. D. W. HILL (Rickmansworth)
White & Red Flag.

It is impossible to begin this new season with the usual message of welcome. No doubt many, if not most, of us have already met at one or more of the Olympian football struggles which have been staged at our Stadium since July 31st. But a whetted blade is the sharper for it. This afternoon is one that all of Arsenal count as a prelude to our enjoyment of the next eight months.

The layout of the above teamsheet departs from our usual pattern. Next Saturday we will revert to the style of yore. The reason? One of you ; using great pains, persuasive argument, a pair of scissors, an old programme, paper and gum ; sent this layout to me towards the end of last season. Summer trials and discussion reveal two schools of opinion. One dislikes it, the other favours its permanent adoption for our programme. Therefore the issue is put straight to you—the Arsenal public. Old style? New style? I will count a vote of all communications received (on a post card please) before we travel north on Friday, August 20th. Use of the telephone will **NOT** record a vote. The result will be published and discussed in a future issue and should the majority desire a change the thing is as good as done.

The Handbook will be on sale for the home fixtures with STOKE CITY (Aug. 25th) and MANCHESTER UNITED (Aug. 28th). No orders can be entertained by post although it is hoped to resume this service one day.

A warm word here of welcome to the bumper crop of new young faces to the red and white of Arsenal. May success with us be their lot ! Full details will be found in the Handbook and will be repeated in an early programme.

The boys will be out soon now and our cheers will sound the start of the season's overture. Let us settle down and watch for points and give this new layout a really good test. Surely even the most rabid fan must be trying to watch all twenty-two players this afternoon !

It is good to be back and met together once more. On behalf of all at Arsenal I wish to say that, win, lose or draw, every single person in or connected with the teams or the Stadium, are out to give of their very best to complete your personal pleasure during the coming season.

" MARKSMAN."

SATURDAY, 14th AUGUST   Kick off 3.15 p.m

PRACTICE MATCH.   Reds v. Whites

Admission 1/- (Tax Exempt) Stands Extra.   Proceeds to Charity.

The programme for my first game for Arsenal, a practice match at Highbury, when I shared the goalkeeping duties with Ted Platt.

Action during the practice match, as Tommy Vallance challenges me for a high ball.

I was playing in the Eastern Counties League, but we had a friendly one Saturday at Chippenham in Wiltshire, about an hour and a half away on the train. After we boarded the train the waiters came round and served boiled fish to everybody. I didn't mind fried fish, but had never eaten boiled fish in my life. George Meale, who used to be a full-back with Arsenal, was the third team manager and I told him I could only eat a couple of bits of toast and a cup of tea. When we reached Chippenham I was starving. At the station there was a confectionary shop, so I bought a couple of Mars bars and put them in my cap as we went onto the field. When I didn't have anything to do in goal I stood munching these bars. At half-time George asked me what I was doing with my hands and mouth. I told him as I was starving and couldn't eat the fish, so I had to have something. On the Monday morning, George reported me for misconduct and I was summoned to see Mr Whittaker. When I explained to him what happened he said he would instruct, in future, Mr Meale, or whoever was in charge of the third team when we played away, that I was to have chicken. We travelled all over the east of England, to Norwich, Bury St Edmunds, and Ipswich, so I always ate chicken and the rest had boiled fish. I don't think George Meale liked it very much, we didn't always see eye to eye, unlike Mr Whittaker. I'm not sure the other players were too happy either, having to watch me munch away at chicken on the train.

In February 1949, I was chosen to play for the first team at Swindon in a friendly match, as both sides were out of the FA Cup and George Swindon and Ted Platt were injured. Tom Whittaker called me and said, 'I'm giving you a chance today Norman, I know you don't get many, but you're playing in the first team.' So, as a twenty-year-old playing for the first team, it was a great thrill to run out of the tunnel behind so many household names. We beat them 4 – 1 with goals from Reg Lewis and Ian McPherson and two from Dougie Lishman. I think I had a pretty decent game. In the Swindon side at outside right was my old school friend Harry Lunn and we had a good chat after the game. The Arsenal team that day was: Uprichard, Smith, Scott, Forbes, Leslie Compton, Macauley, Vallance, Lishman, Lewis, Bryn Jones, McPherson.

The big stars in the main trained at Highbury, we in the third team and the youngsters trained at Hendon. They provided lunch for us after training and I would say they were the most professional club I played for and provided me with the springboard for greater things. There were over fifty professionals at the club at the time, and a huge staff. As keepers, we all got on well and there was never any animosity. The stars in those days were Ronnie Rooke (centre forward), Don Roper (outside right), Jimmy Logie (inside right), Dougie Lishman (inside left), Tommy Vallance (outside left), Archie Macauley (right half), Leslie Compton, who played in various positions, and Alex Forbes and Laurie Scott

Marrying my biggest fan, Lily, in January 1949 at Richview Presbyterian church, Belfast.

(right back). I didn't come into contact much with them, although I was involved in a commercial with Ronnie Rooke once. Ronnie had a very fierce shot on him and hit the ball to the right hand corner of the goal and I dived, got a hand on it and saved it. That upset the advertisers as I wasn't supposed to stop it and Tom Whittaker, who was watching, said, 'Don't stop them Norman, you might hurt your hand!'

Back in Ireland I had seen a pretty girl called Elizabeth Gourley watching a game at Distillery and vowed to meet her. When we first moved across to England, Elizabeth and I lived in the same house in digs at Plimsoll Road, a stone's throw from Highbury, but slept in separate rooms, as one did in those days. Nine months later, on 29 January 1949, I married Lily at the tender age of twenty at Richview Presbyterian church, Donegal Road, Belfast. Elizabeth was a year younger than me and my best man was my uncle Bertie. After a reception at Sandy Row Orange Hall, we had our honeymoon in Dublin and when we returned to Plimsoll Road slept in the same bedroom! Tom Whittaker managed to get a job for Lily working as a stitcher for Sid Godfrey, one of the directors, who owned a linen factory in North London.

Chapter Four

Swindon Calling

I had been at Arsenal for just over a year when in November 1949, Tom Whittaker called me into the office one day and introduced me to Louis Page, manager of Third Division South Swindon Town. Tom said, 'Norman, although we know you are full of promise I'd like you to go to Swindon Town. Mr Page has two teams but only one goalkeeper as the first team keeper Frank Boulton (who was also an ex-Arsenal player) has broken his leg. I would advise you to go for the simple reason that you will get a game every week, whereas here you'll only get a game every two or three weeks. If anything happens to you, you have my word I'll take you back here for another season at least. They'll pay you £14 a week and £12 in the summer plus your accrued share of benefit' (which was about £187). That represented about a year and eight months at £150 a year benefit from the club and £750 after five years if the club wanted to pay it. Tom's word was his bond as far as I was concerned, he was a fabulous man. Louis Page called him 'the whitest man in the business,' as in those days there was a lot of talk about players being sold in slave markets. As a further illustration of how different football was, I subsequently discovered Swindon did actually have a third keeper, Doug Rylands, but he was on forces duty overseas!

I was getting depressed at Highbury, sitting there watching the first team or reserves, only getting a game in the third team against a club like Cambridge and, with a young son and £4 a week rise, it was a good opportunity for me. I understand Swindon paid a nominal £750 fee for me, but Louis Page and Tom were good friends and went back a long time. Louis played for England alongside Dixie Dean, but I don't know how he became friendly with Tom. I could have gone back to Ireland – I know Linfield would have signed me, as one of the directors told me if I was ever thinking of returning to let him know. He would have fixed me up at Windsor Park, but it would only have been as a last resort.

My first game for Swindon was at Ipswich with the reserves. As I was living in London, I met the other players for the first time at Liverpool Street Station on

Swindon Town manager Louis Page was a big influence on my career.

the Friday night and we stayed overnight at a hotel in Ipswich. It was the best pitch in England at the time and I saved a penalty, we won 3 – 1, and I managed to get a good write-up. Other reserve team games were against Spurs, Cardiff, Swansea and Plymouth Argyle. We won two of these and drew two. After the goalless Plymouth game a reporter wrote, 'Uprichard kept his goal beautifully, saving twice when it seemed that Argyle must score.'

That encouraged me, and I enjoyed myself, making new friends. I finally made my first team debut on Christmas Eve 1949, taking over from Sam Burton when we lost 2 – 1 to Torquay. That season I made five league appearances, the final one being a 5 – 0 drubbing by Nottingham Forest, but I was still learning my trade and biding my time. One of my earliest games was a 0 – 0 draw at Aldershot on New Year's Eve 1949, and reported as follows;

Defences won the day at Aldershot, where there was nothing better than the prodigious feats of Norman Uprichard. The lad didn't need the jesting cry of the crowd, "Up Richard!" to spur him. He was there all the time, tops with magnificently spectacular saves from Mortimore, Hobbs and Cropley that frustrated the Aldershot attackers time and time again.

The following season, 1950–51, followed a similar pattern with an injury to Sam Burton leading to a twelve-game run of appearances, starting on Boxing Day 1950, again with a 1 – 0 defeat at Torquay. I started my run of bad injuries that was to plague me throughout my career at Swindon that season; the worst was at Plymouth in March 1951, who had Gordon Astall of England and Alex Govan, who should have played for Scotland in their side. We led with a 'Garth' Hudson penalty before Astall drove a fierce low ball across my 18-yard line a few minutes before half-time. I ran out and dived to smother it without any thought as to the danger there might be to my life or limbs. Simultaneously, an inside forward called George Willis came thundering in, on my blindside, and hit me in the ribs with his two knees full blast. I was carried off with two broken, and three cracked ribs, and full back Jack Foxton went in goal. I came back and hobbled about on the right wing but we lost 5 – 1. Back at Swindon, I was strapped up like a mummy for about ten weeks, with rolls of 3-inch tape from my stomach to my armpits. When they were taken off my skin was incredibly tender. It had turned red and was covered in sores, which took another three weeks to clear.

Louis Page warned me to be less suicidal, as also did one reporter, 'I wish Uprichard would make discretion the better part of valour when he dives at the feet of forwards and pay more attention to protecting his head. He has had enough bangs on it to last a season or two already.' Some writers began to call me 'Uprichard the Fearless', but I didn't see it like that. Maybe I was just plain mad! If I felt I had a 50–50 chance of clutching, or smothering, a ball before it was rammed into the net by some big, powerful, ugly centre forward, I just went hell for leather. In a split second I didn't have time to think about the possibility of getting injured. That's probably why during the course of my career I had practically every bone in my body broken, though over time I eventually learnt how to minimise risks. For example, after a while I would fist the ball away if I was under pressure, after being bundled into the net with the ball a few times. You have to bear in mind that goalkeepers didn't receive anything like the protection they do now by referees.

You can see in the photo of Tommy Lawton I was given at the St Peter's dinner that he is sportingly holding back where, if he had followed through, both the ball and my head would probably have ended up in the net. I had heard that Tommy, when about to connect with the ball, used to shout to the opposing keeper with great humour but also great confidence, 'Pick it out'. More often than not, the poor goalkeeper found himself doing precisely that, with the ball in the back of the net. I don't remember Tommy ever shouting that to me, but I only played against him in his later days when his razor-sharp timing had blunted slightly.

Jackie Milburn was another who used restraint, as forwards also had to exercise split-second judgement. I rated Jackie not only among the greatest centre forwards I played against, but also among the greatest footballing gentlemen it was my privilege to play against. In a game soon after returning from one of my countless injuries, I went up for a high cross in the first minute. I flinched, waiting for the crashing challenge to come from Jackie, for I was off the ground and my arms and legs were high as I caught the ball. But Jackie stood off and shouted, 'Get rid of it lad'. A great sportsman, it was his way of saying, 'Welcome back'.

Our own centre forward, Maurice Owen from Abingdon near Oxford, was in the same category. During my Swindon days, Maurice was rated among the three best centre forwards in England. Wolves wanted to sign him, amongst others; they offered £14,000, but he was very happy with his Swindon 'family' and chose to remain at the County Ground. Other players I admired were Newcastle's Scottish forward Bobby 'Dazzler' Mitchell and the brilliant Wolves wingers Johnny Hancocks and Jimmy Mullen.

It was only during the 1951–52 season that I was finally able to take my chance and gain the number one position from big Sam. I went to the County Ground for the fourth game of the season at the end of August 1951 to watch a derby match against Bristol Rovers. When I reached the ground, Louis Page told me to get changed as Sam was in bed with the flu. I realised that fate caused by injury had again thrust me into the limelight. Sam was a local hero, Swindon born and bred, 'Strong in the arm, weak in the head', they used to say, but a fine keeper and a hell of a nice fella. As I ran out the announcer said over the tannoy, Sam was indisposed and replaced by me. I could hear the groan of disappointment go round the ground. Bristol Rovers were a very useful side and hit us with everything. I particularly remember how dangerous Geoff Bradford was but we drew 0 – 0, and the groans turned to cheers and I had a blinder. I came off the park to a standing ovation and from that day I was first team choice at Swindon, despite intense competition from Sam. The local paper reported, 'It's this rivalry for senior status that puts the pep into a team. Swindon would be in a more satisfactory position than they are today if more of their first team positions were as keenly duplicated as that of goalkeeper.'

So I established myself that season, when we had high hopes of improving on our lowly position of seventeenth in the league. In the event, we managed to nudge up one place to sixteenth, at least it was in the right direction! With forty-two league and nine cup games, Sam only took over when I was injured, which became a recurrent feature of my career. Indeed, I eventually became known to the sports writers as 'the unluckiest goalkeeper in the business'. Whilst realising I had to keep learning, I started to feel that I had at last arrived. I also began to wonder if I might be chosen to play for my country. I knew I had some way to go, even though the international selectors had apparently not managed to solve the goalkeeping problem which had plagued them since the end of the war, or at least since the playing days of Hugh Kelly and, in particular, of the great Tommy Breene. My chance came in October 1951, when I made my international debut against Scotland, but more about that later.

Swindon embarked on a nine game FA Cup run in the 1951–52 season which brought much needed cash into the club. We beat Bedford 2 – 0 in the first round and then were drawn against Torquay. After two hectic draws home and away, we finally defeated them 3 – 1 at Bristol City's ground. In the third round we secured a draw in January 1952 at Division Two leaders Cardiff City with a Maurice Owen goal in front of 40,000, winning the replay 1 – 0. We were lucky though, as City had most of the play, but Maurice scored the winning goal nine minutes from the end of extra time. I had what was described as 'the game of my life' but, with a little more luck City's forwards, particularly Evans and Grant, might have scored a goal apiece.

Teams need a bit of luck in a cup run, and we then drew 1 – 1 with Stoke City at home in the next round. Sammy Smyth, the Northern Ireland inside forward, scored for them. In the replay, two days later, we beat them 1 – 0 with a goal from Willie Millar.

The teams for the two ties were:

Swindon: Uprichard, Hunt, May, Kay, Hudson, Gray, Lunn, Onslow (Millar came in for the replay), Owen, Betteridge, Bain.
Stoke: Herod, Mould, McCue, Martin, Mountford, Kirton, Malkin, Bowyer, Sellars, Smyth, Oscroft.

We were finally defeated 3 – 1 on 23 February in the fifth round by Luton, who included Bud Aherne, formerly of Belfast Celtic, at left back. We had however, reached the last sixteen, quite an achievement for a Division Three outfit! The Stoke matches were, at the time, the highlight of my short career at Swindon and I credit Louis Page for more astute advice he gave me before the first encounter. As one reporter noted,

> Maybe the brilliance of Uprichard disheartened Stoke and made them wonder just what they had to do to score. The Irishman's superb form right from the first four minutes, when he was stretched to the limit, was enough to take the heart out of the forwards. Uprichard is only twenty three, but there was a seasoned head behind his display – manager Louis Page's. During his pre-match talk the Town's chief warned Uprichard about his occasional failing of getting caught in two minds, as he was when Cardiff scored their goal at Ninian Park.

Above and below: Two action shots in goal for Swindon from the 1951–52 FA Cup replay against Cardiff City at the County Ground, which we won 1 – 0 after extra time.

I remember Louis told me, 'Make up your mind, what you are going to do, and then stick to it whether you are right or wrong.' Sound advice and I remembered that for the remainder of my career. I was still learning my trade at the time and even now keepers find one of the most difficult decisions is whether to stick or come off their line. Louis told me to be decisive and I would gain the confidence of my defence.

Financially our cup success meant a huge amount to the club. My only regret was when we met Stoke at home in our drawn first encounter, the club had to turn away about £2,000 for this glamorous all-ticket match and we broke the ground record. Our ground capacity was limited to 28,500 for safety reasons and we were sad to learn that 47,000 spectators wanted to attend. We also heard that the directors, only five months previously, had been paying our wages out of their own pockets, mainly because it was their policy to plough profits back into ground improvements and buying properties to house players. It was also their policy to reject financially tempting transfer offers in the interests of the club. At the same time, they would never deny a player the opportunity to better himself if he could, as I was to find out. At the time of the Stoke match, Louis Page said to the press:

> Our common accent is on team work without any accepted stars. Two players would, however draw five figure fees if the club let them go – Norman Uprichard and Maurice Owen. Uprichard is the best goalkeeper in the Third Division and not far from being the best in any division.

Needless to say, that sort of compliment from Mr Page gave me great pleasure, but also made me ambitious to leave Swindon for a higher level. When I did eventually leave, it was with Mr Page's blessing.

In March 1952, soon after the cup run, we played a league game at Torquay. In the first half I dived at Tommy Northcott's feet and got a terrific kick in the head. I was groggy but the trainer poured water down my back – we weren't too scientific in those days! The next thing I knew, a ball came in from the right wing from about fifty yards and went in the far corner of the net. I never moved and the trainer carried me off. I lay on the dressing room bench until full-time while Harry Kaye went in goal. At the start of the second half I returned for a while but was suffering from double vision and Harry went back in goal when we were 4 – 0 down. Harry May also had a turn in goal, but in the event we crashed 9 – 0, which is still Swindon's heaviest league defeat. My reward was a spell of three days in hospital. At least we made further progress in the league, finishing in tenth position.

There was a tremendous spirit at Swindon amongst the players and supporters and we made sure we had some fun along the way. We came in for training one day when Sam Burton and Maurice Owen, two real characters and head cases – as bad as me – took Harry Kaye's bike, got some streamers that were still all over the place from the last match, tied them round his bike and hoisted it up the flagpole on top of the stand. When Harry came out he looked for his bike everywhere and we said, 'What's that up there?' He looked up and couldn't believe where his bike had ended up. It was always taken in good heart and Maurice, Sam and I got up to all sorts of practical jokes.

There was a big hut at the side of the stand which was the club's own recreation club. It didn't sell alcohol, but we often went there after training and played darts or snooker instead of walking the streets. It helped develop a really close bond with the other players. As well as Maurice and Sam, I remember Jimmy Bain (outside left), big George 'Garth' Hudson (centre-half), George Hunt (right back), Harry May (left back) and Harry Kaye (left half). Cliff Walcroft, South of England snooker champion, taught me to play snooker at Swindon, teaching me all the safety shots, etc.

Harry Lunn arrived at Swindon from Notts County before me. He had by then become a fine player, and a very fast, direct, winger. He should have been capped for Northern Ireland and in my estimation was as good as, if not a better direct winger than, Billy Bingham. He scored some fine goals for us and I remember in particular one which earned us a 1 – 1 draw against Newport County. The report linked us together nicely,

> Two Irishmen gain Town a point. Newport County played much better football and Swindon's run of six games without defeat was extended to seven only by the superb goalkeeping of Uprichard and the incisiveness and opportunism of Lunn. Uprichard had one of those days which send opposing forwards grey with despair. His anticipation was uncanny.

Harry and I were always close friends and many a time we adjourned for a couple of pints to talk about the old days. When Harry got married to a local Swindon girl, I was chief usher on his side. I was responsible for making sure everyone had a drink at the reception and of course made sure I had one myself. I must have taken my responsibilities very seriously as I managed to get pissed as a pudding, and when I went to the toilet hit my head and fell asleep in the bath. I had a sore head for more than one reason.

It was certainly true to say the game was harder, and the pitches were softer in those days. I remember matches where the ground staff were out whitewashing the lines for the second half. Playing at Newport County, in one game, the mud was about 12 inches deep in the goalmouth. You'd have to be mad, or Irish, or both, to be a goalkeeper in those conditions.

Chapter Five

The Big Time at Pompey

I was playing very well at Swindon and was classed by the press as one of the three top goalkeepers in England, the other two being Bert Williams of Wolves and Sam Bartram. The press also indicated that there were at least three Division One clubs with goalkeeping problems watching me. I felt there was nothing I couldn't get to, as I was very agile at the time and thought a transfer must be in the offing, and a chance to play at the highest level. When the move came, it all happened very quickly. Unknown to me, Eddie Lever, the Portsmouth manager, had watched me play at Windsor Park in October 1952 against England and was also at the 1 – 1 draw with Scotland at Hampden Park on Wednesday, 5 November 1952. On the Thursday night I was told at our house in Swindon that Louis Page wanted to see me and Lily at the ground, which was a bit of an inconvenience as I had planned to go out for a pint or two! Louis introduced me to Mr Lever, who I had actually seen on the same train back from Glasgow, and Phil Harris, the secretary. I shook hands with them and Louis asked me how I would like to play for First Division Portsmouth as Ernie Butler, the number one keeper at Pompey had broken his hand. I said, 'Great, as long as the wages were all right, etc.' They said they couldn't pay me anything the FA didn't allow, although they did give Lily a tenner to buy herself something and I also had a £10 signing on fee. I was Eddie's first signing. I understand the fee was £9,500, a record fee for Swindon. My wages were good and I received my share of the accrued benefit from the club as well, about £450 less tax of course.

After returning from our international headquarters in Bangor for the England game in October 1952, I only played three more times for Swindon. My last game was a 6 – 3 home defeat against Crystal Palace on 1 November 1952. Maybe it was a good time to move on! I had played seventy-three games for Swindon and won five full international caps. At the same time, I felt more than a little sad to be leaving Swindon. Louis Page had been a supportive manager but he was given little money to strengthen the squad and also went at the end of that season. I had

Eddie Lever, Portsmouth manager, who I enjoyed playing for.

three very happy years there, I liked the club and the people, practically everyone in Swindon knew me, and they were invariably friendly and generous. We were all one big, happy family and they had facilities no other club had. I will always remember that Swindon Town made me as a footballer. Had I not been sent there by Tom Whittaker, it's quite possible my career would have stalled.

I travelled down to Portsmouth on the Friday after signing and stayed in a house near the ground with a couple by the name of Mr and Mrs Trout. My debut was against Tottenham Hotspur at Fratton Park on Saturday 8 November 1952. When I arrived at the ground there was a telegram on my seat from Tom Whittaker, 'Best of luck with your new club.' I thought that was fabulous.

We beat them 2 – 1 with a 20-yard strike from Peter Harris, and a second from Duggie Reid ten minutes into the second half. I didn't really have a lot to do, but managed to concede an own goal with about ten minutes to go. I dived for the ball from Dennis Uphill, stopped it and as I was falling, the other hand hit it into the net. So I scored a goal for Spurs on my debut. At the final whistle my opposite number Ted Ditchburn, a very fine goalkeeper and a gentleman as well, ran up and congratulated me as we left the field together. Thirteen of the players were internationals and the crowd numbered over 40,000, so it was a huge step up for me.

Early days at Portsmouth. I already have my right arm in a sling as a result of the clash with Derek Dooley in November 1952. In digs with the Trout family, who provided accommodation for over twenty years to Portsmouth players.

The Teams were:

Portsmouth: Uprichard, Gunter, Stephen, Scoular, Froggatt, Dickinson, Harris, Mundy, Reid, Phillips, Gailliard.
Tottenham: Ditchburn, Ramsey, Willis, Nicholson, Clarke, Burgess, Walters, Uphill, Duquemin, Baily, Medley.

Pompey had been Football League champions as recently as 1948–49 and 1949–50, and I realised that I had finally reached the big time. That feeling was reinforced when I sat in the dressing room and looked around me. Our half-back line was Jimmy Scoular, a captain in every sense of the word, Jackie Froggatt, an England international and strong in the air, and Jimmy Dickinson, who had no superior when it came to the precision pass and deadly tackle.

Telegram from Tom Whittaker wishing me well on my debut for Portsmouth dated 8 November 1952.

My second game was at Hillsborough against Sheffield Wednesday, who were a good side. According to the press reports it was one of the best matches ever seen at Hillsborough. We were winning 4 – 3, with goals from Albert Mundy, Len Phillips, and Peter Harris, with a minute to go, when Renfrew Froggatt, the England inside forward and a cousin of Jackie Froggatt, came through with the ball. I dived at his feet and got the ball. Following up behind was big centre forward Derek Dooley, who came flying in. The ball and my hands were protecting my head, but he crunched two knuckles so hard with his boot that I couldn't get my right hand into my jacket after the game, it was so swollen and painful. He could easily have pulled out, but never apologised, or sent me a letter, nor did Sheffield Wednesday, despite it clearly being a bad injury. At least I stopped them scoring! I always felt it ironic that three months later Dooley broke his leg in a collision with Preston goalkeeper George Thompson, which finished his career.

I travelled back to Swindon, as I hadn't yet moved to Portsmouth. The following day, a friend drove me to Portsmouth hospital where an X-ray examination confirmed that my two knuckles were shattered and that I'd be out for about six weeks. My injury jinx had struck again. It was Boxing Day before I returned to play out the remainder of the season – bar the final two games. However, whenever I punched the ball or flicked it over the bar, the pain was excruciating, and the hand blew up like a balloon. I knew it wasn't right, especially with the injury I sustained with my finger as a child, but nobody likes to be out of the game for long and I wasn't going to admit I had a problem. We ended the season in fifteenth position and I also played in the home international against Wales on 15 April.

Chapter Six

My 'Lost' Season

In my heart of hearts I knew I was struggling to overcome the hand injury suffered at Sheffield Wednesday. I can truthfully say until that stage of my career I never failed to use my bad hand when it was needed, and suffered in silence. However, I also knew the moment of truth was probably not far away. My hand wasn't really fit for the first game of the 1953–54 season, a 3 – 1 reverse at Anfield against Liverpool. I came through it without too much trouble, but as a precaution, Charlie Dore came in for me at home to Sheffield United. In our third match towards the end of August 1953 we lost 4 – 3 to Chelsea at Stamford Bridge, and in the closing minutes I jumped to catch a pile-driver from Jim Lewis and once more the pain shot through my entire right arm. My knuckles were smashed again and I knew I was in real trouble. A Harley Street specialist told me kindly but firmly that I must not touch a ball again for at least six months. His exact words were, 'If you do, you will never play again.' They were the most frightening words I ever had to listen to. I knew he was right, but felt very depressed about it all. I went to hospital where my hand was submerged in a wax bath and it gradually formed like a glove to protect it. The news soon swept through the club and everyone was very kind to me. Without the support and encouragement of my friends, including the press, I might never have emerged from the long dark tunnel I had just entered after four wonderful years. Eddie Lever saw to it that I didn't get bored and still trained daily, playing in an outfield position, and did some scouting for the club and I even looked after one of the Junior sides. Strangely, he bought Ted Platt to replace me, who I had competed with at Highbury when I first joined Arsenal.

The trainers played their part too. They were Jimmy Nichol, Billy Wright and Jimmy Stewart, a hard man from Scotland – the general who supervised the others and would make you run all day if he could. Stewart was the trainer at Blackpool when Peter Doherty joined them, and is credited with making him into a better player. Peter was a very clever footballer, but early in his career wouldn't always get

The broken hand in a sling as I'm pictured in the dressing room.

Keeping myself fit by running round the track at Fratton Park under the watchful eye of Jimmy Nichol, Billy Wright and Jimmy Stewart.

rid of the ball, so in friendly matches Jimmy told the opposition to hit him so that he would release the ball earlier. Jimmy said that turned him into a better player, as he got clouted so much he would get to know when to release the ball earlier.

Before my second visit to the specialist six months later, I was more nervous than ever I had felt before a big match. My career and livelihood was in the balance and his verdict was some improvement and there was no X-ray evidence of permanent injury. However, I was to rest for a further three months. Again, everyone at the club helped keep my spirits up until the end of my 'lost' season and return visit to Harley Street. I had been able to exercise my hand by squeezing the inside of a golf ball to get the flexibility back, which was very beneficial. I was told there had been more improvement but was still not allowed to touch a ball. So I kept myself physically fit and continued to exercise the hand during the close season, and it gradually felt stronger. At the end of June 1954, I revisited the specialist with Eddie Lever. In his consulting room the surgeon, at first very gently and then somewhat less gently, turned my hand while he looked me straight in the face to see if there was any reaction. Then he shook me by the hand and said, 'You can keep goal again.' Those five words meant the world to me and I was close to tears. Due to the orthopaedic skill of the surgeon, the kindness of Eddie Lever, and support of countless people, I had won the greatest battle of my career. I felt so relieved, but still had to punch my first shot for almost a year, which I managed to do the very next day without any pain.

When the practice matches for the start of the 1954–55 season began, the club devised a rubber glove with a sponge pad inside to compensate for the two 'lost' knuckles. I have to confess it was never quite right, but the glove did help to cushion the impact when I punched the ball. I always tried to catch the ball instead of punching it after that. Most goalkeeping gloves from that era were pretty primitive, a far cry from the advanced techniques they put into designing gloves nowadays. They were usually only worn when the ball was wet, and they were made of wool or cord, whichever was better, as the woollen ones quickly became wet and heavy. It was Jersey wool until the mid to late 1950s, when they were made of a newer, lightweight material.

I was back in goal for the first match, a big upset, as in August 1954 we beat Manchester United 3 – 1 at Old Trafford with goals from Gordon Dale, Jackie Henderson and an own goal. I had a blinder, saving them from all angles and will always treasure the report of the game, which was headlined, 'The man who refused to give in' and reported,

Norman Uprichard is back – back to the form the Irish selectors want to see. Playing against Manchester United he was in great form. The south coast club caused a sensation with their 3 – 1 win over the much fancied northerners.

At home with Lily and our son Stephen. Note the old style leather football is the centre of attraction.

With Lily and Stephen at the 1953 Portsmouth Club Christmas party.

Practising in the gym with Stephen at Portsmouth.

My mother Henrietta with baby
Pauline, and Stephen.

Norman takes a large share of the credit. His comeback is a story of pluck and
determination. It is almost a year to the day since he injured his hand against
Chelsea. To Portsmouth it meant signing a new keeper – Ted Platt from Arsenal.
But you've got to give Portsmouth a pat on the back for their treatment of Norman.
Most clubs would have cut their losses and written him off. Instead they arranged
a series of appointments with a top specialist. Special hot-wax baths in the winter
gave him a faint hope. To keep fit he played centre forward in practice games.
Instead of going off in the summer he got down to more training. Every day he
reported to Fratton Park. He was a lone figure running the track. Often members
of the staff gave him mild goalkeeping practice. Sometimes Eddie Lever took over
the role of a shooting forward. As the first game against United progressed it was
obvious his skill was not impaired. Matt Busby was among those greatly impressed
by Uprichard's showing.

Matt Busby was reported as saying, 'You'd never have thought he had a serious
hand injury. His fielding of the ball was clean and confident. A great comeback
by a man who just wouldn't give in.' Those words meant a huge amount to me

The Portsmouth team is introduced to Field Marshal Montgomery at Fratton Park during the 1954–55 season.

and my confidence, especially coming from a defeated manager, but Matt was a very big-hearted and generous individual.

The teams were:

Portsmouth: Uprichard, Wilson, Mansell, Phillips, Reid, Pickett, Harris, Gordon, Henderson, Barnard, Dale.
Manchester United: Wood, Foulkes, Byrne, Whitefoot, Chilton, Edwards, Berry, Blanchflower, Webster, Viollet, Rowley.

That season I had an equally good game at Everton in a 3 – 2 victory. I rate Goodison Park as one of my lucky grounds. Everton brought over a large number of supporters from Dublin every other week, and all these Dubliners knew I was from the north and, being a Protestant, would give me stick. If I brought off a good save I'd turn round and give them the two fingers. Peter Farrell, the captain

Portsmouth First Team from that wonderful 1954–55 season. Back row: Tommy McGhee, Jack Mansell, Phil Gunter, myself, Duggie Reid, Reg Pickett, Jackie Henderson. Front row: Peter Harris, Johnny Gordon, Jimmy Dickinson, Derek Rees, Gordon Dale.

and left half, Jimmy O'Neill the goalie, and Tommy Eglington were all from Dublin. They were very good friends and I always got on well with them and we'd have a laugh about the Irish supporters. I also enjoyed playing at Anfield, where the crowd, whilst Liverpool supporters to the backbone, appreciated opposition goalies who brought off a few good saves by applauding you.

We played Bolton mid-winter when the pitch had degenerated into a sea of mud. Both the game and light were fading to a close when I placed the ball for a goal kick and, as I had a groin strain, asked Duggie Reid to take it. He ran up and miskicked it straight to Nat Lofthouse, who coolly lobbed the ball over my head into an empty net. Nat said to me, 'Thank you very much Norman and the same to Duggie. I don't get many gifts nowadays!'

There were many other special games I recall from the 1954–55 season, when Pompey had an excellent side. We were still in with a chance of the title at Easter but with just one win in six matches, fell away to finish third in

Behind a shot from Wolves forward Roy Swinbourne (extreme left) during the famous heat-wave epic at Fratton Park in August 1955.

Division One, just four points behind champions Chelsea. We played very open, attractive football, and Eddie Lever was able to pick a settled side, which made an enormous amount of difference. I only missed one game, which was due to an international call-up, and managed to keep ten clean sheets, conceding sixty-two goals in the league, which was less than Chelsea and Wolves, who finished in second place. We regularly had gates of about 35,000 and our biggest win was in December 1954, when we thrashed FA Cup holders West Brom 6 – 1 at Fratton Park, with goals from Henderson, Harris (2), Barnard, Gordon and an own goal. The conditions were quite muddy and apart from the first minute, when I had to save from Johnny Nicholls, and the last minute, when Ronnie Allen beat me with a fine shot which went in off the crossbar, I didn't have a lot to do.

At the start of the following season in August 1955 we defeated Wolves 2 – 1 at Fratton Park when they were at their peak, with goals from Peter Harris and Johnny Gordon. Peter Campling, who later helped expose the football bribery scandal in 1964, wrote,

Diving at the feet of Tommy Lawton during a 3 – 1 victory over Arsenal in September 1955. This was the great Tommy's last match at Highbury.

Watching as a diving effort from Derek Tapscott sails over the bar. Duggie Reid (No. 5) looks on.

Two further shots from the famous victory at Highbury in September 1955, as I manage to thwart further efforts from the Arsenal attack.

Shepherding the ball out of play with Derek Tapscott and Jimmy Dickinson either side of me, Portsmouth *v.* Arsenal, September 1955.

Some of soccer's missing millions should have seen this heat wave epic. It was football at its best. Thousands of programmes fanned the crowd, but on the field the pace never let up. Wolves fought to the last gasp for the equaliser. Little Johnny Hancocks might easily have got it when two of his terrific shots were saved by Uprichard. Portsmouth deserved their win, but what a battle it was. First Bert Williams would be leaping to save, then Uprichard would have the crowd cheering.

Then we had a memorable game at Highbury in September 1955, beating an Arsenal side 3 – 1 that included Tommy Lawton, Derek Tapscott and Don Roper. A report of the game stated, 'The suicide saves of the man with the padded glove, Norman Uprichard, made Highbury gasp between their cheers for Portsmouth's classic football.' I said at the time in an interview, 'Upon my comeback I wondered if I could keep my nerve. I need not have worried. Wearing a sponge-padded glove allows one to punch the ball without feeling a thing. The only concession I make is instinctively to hug the ball to me with my injured right hand while I throw out my left to keep out the oncoming boots.' I got through about a dozen of those special gloves every season, but without them I would never have been able to carry on.

In October 1955, a few seconds after the beginning of our home game to Tottenham, there was an incident that could have been disastrous and embarrassing. Before the start of every match the crowd used to shower me with sweets and bars of chocolate as I ran into my goalmouth. I was still picking them up and putting them into my cap when I heard the ball smash against the underside of the crossbar. It actually crossed the line but the referee missed it. I hadn't heard him blow the whistle for the start of the game and was totally oblivious that Dave Dunmore had burst through and shot. We went on to win 4 – 1 and it became a great joke with the Pompey players. I don't think they would have enjoyed it so much if the ref had realised it had gone over the line! It was quite an eventful game, as later I dived at the feet of their centre forward, Len Duquemin, and the ball hit me in the face and temporarily knocked me out. I had long realised that you had to be tough as well as mad to make the grade as a goalkeeper in professional football.

At half-time in the game against Huddersfield at Fratton Park in December 1955, I came off clutching an outsize Christmas stocking full of sweets, books and games for my son. A fan had left it in the goalmouth with a note, 'To Stephen, Merry Christmas.' When I joined Pompey I used to give all the sweets to Stephen, but after a while the players insisted I share them. It became quite common to dish them out at half-time and occasionally to the opposition if they were not giving me a hard time. Barry Harris, the sailor mascot got a few as well; I could have opened a sweet shop there were so many. After a while, the kindness of Pompey supporters matched that of Swindon, which is a huge compliment after the generosity of those from the County Ground.

In February 1956, I played in the first ever floodlit League game when we were defeated 2 – 0 by Newcastle at Fratton Park. I remember, it was a freezing cold night and I wore long 'pants' to keep warm and protect myself against the icy conditions. Against the run of play, Bill Curry beat me with a cross/shot after half an hour and Vic Keeble sealed their victory eleven minutes from time.

We finished the season in mid-table, so there were some signs of more difficult times ahead. I played forty-one games, the same as the previous season, injury free, but it was not to last.

In 1956–57 I was again plagued with injuries, which restricted me to twenty-two appearances. It had actually started quite well, as during the close season we played Holland in Rotterdam and the press generally agreed we were unlucky to be beaten 3 – 2. However, it was a difficult year for us. We were never higher than fifth from bottom and seemed doomed to relegation, until a run of four matches yielded seven points enabling us to finish nineteenth.

A spectacular save during Pompey's 3 – 2 victory at Blackpool on Boxing Day 1955.

Another match at Old Trafford against Manchester United in October 1957 sticks out. Apart from a Southern Floodlit Cup tie against Charlton, it was my first game of the season, taking over from Alan Barnett after another injury. It also marked the debut of Derek Dougan, a shrewd signing by Eddie Lever from Distillery. Whilst the 'Doog' didn't score, he played a part in the first and third goals scored by Jackie Henderson and Peter Harris. Ron Newman also found the back of the net, to secure a famous 3 – 0 victory. Early on I had to make a couple of saves from Liam Whelan, then late in the game, from Eddie Colman and Mark Jones, but the defence held firm, superbly marshalled by Jimmy Dickinson and Cyril Rutter.

The teams were:

Portsmouth: Uprichard, Gunter, Wilson, Albury, Rutter, Dickinson, Harris, Gordon, Dougan, Henderson, Newman.
Manchester United: Wood, Foulkes, Jones, Colman, Blanchflower, McGuinness, Berry, Whelan, Dawson, Viollet, Pegg.

The playing staff from the 1955–56 season.

First Team 1956–57 season. Back row: Tommy McGhee, Cyril Rutter, myself, Mike Barnard, Phil Gunter. Front row: Peter Harris, Johnny Gordon, Jimmy Dickinson, John Phillips, Jackie Henderson, Gordon Dale.

Keeping the Manchester United attack at bay, as Pompey secure a fine win at Old Trafford in October 1957.

In our last game of the season we won the Southern Floodlit Cup by beating Reading 2 – 0. It was a midweek knock-out trophy played mainly between clubs from the south-east. However, our experienced players were not adequately replaced and we clung on to our First Division place on goal average at the expense of Sunderland, but at least I managed to get thirty-six games under my belt.

When I was at Portsmouth, my mother sold out in Ireland and came over to live with us. She met this bloke called Stan who was from Portadown, which is five miles from Lurgan. He managed a small holiday camp called Nortons on the Isle of Wight, and offered my mother a job there. She wasn't doing anything in Portsmouth at the time, so took the job and worked there for about three years. My wages at Pompey were £20 during the season and £17 in the summer, so through her I also got a job there during the summer as a porter or anything that needed doing. I had three months in the summer doing nothing and you can only play so much golf, snooker and darts. I was never an indoor type of person, so it appealed to me. I would have a few bevvies at the end of the night, inevitably get pissed up on Scrumpy at least once out there, come home once or twice a week to see the wife and kids, make sure they were all right and give them some money. For a couple of summers I also worked at a laundrette owned by one of the directors at Portsmouth with Tommy McGhee, our full back.

Chapter Seven

Winter of Discontent

Eddie Lever was an absolute gentleman. He was too nice a man to be a football manager really; he was an ex-school teacher. He was not a particularly astute tactician, and he used to say before a match, 'Fight and chase, fight for every ball, chase every ball,' which was more or less his team talk. To be fair, he did go to the World Cup Finals in 1954 with Jimmy Nichol to study the way foreign teams played and also their training methods. He introduced more variety and ball work into the training and more of a short than long ball game as a direct result. Some of the players also started to wear the continental style lightweight boots to good effect, most notably Jackie Henderson, Peter Harris, Len Phillips and Jack Mansell.

During my 'lost' season with Portsmouth I was kept as happy as possible and treated wonderfully by everyone, especially Eddie. After my comeback, and return for the seasons 1954–56, when I was also first choice for Northern Ireland, I could never for a moment imagine I would ever be either unhappy or discontented at Pompey. As at Swindon, we were all one big happy family. After five years at the club I received a benefit of £750; they were allowed to give you £150 per year. Jackie Henderson told me to invest it, so I took his advice and it went straight into my bank account.

That all turned sour when the board sacked Eddie in April 1958. He had been connected with the club for nearly thirty years, but after our poor season the club felt it was time for a change. In June 1958, Freddie Cox, an Arsenal winger in my time there, was appointed manager. He'd done reasonably well just along the coast at Bournemouth, where they pulled off a giant-killing feat by beating Spurs in the FA Cup in 1956–57. Cox arrived sold on the idea of the various continental formations, particularly 4–2–4, and tried overnight to impose this on a team, like all other British teams at the time, brought up on 2–3–5. The players could not adapt to the dramatic formation change, nor did many wish to, except some youngsters keen to impress. His persistent arrogance meant he was rapidly destroying a decent team but he was unable to see it and Pompey were relegated in his first season. The board of course bought into his views, but two years later were forced to change their minds, when Cox was sacked in February 1961 with the club heading towards another disastrous relegation. But by then the damage had been done.

We had some great players in our team – Jimmy Scoular, right half for Scotland, was the hardest man I ever came across. I was glad I was in his team; he used to give me a real bollocking if I let in a soft goal. Others included Jimmy Dickinson, forty-eight caps for England, Peter Harris (outside right), Len Phillips (inside right), Jackie Henderson (centre forward), Gordon Dale (outside left), Phil Gunter (right back), and Jackie Mansell (left back). It was a very good team, very hard to beat, but then different players arrived and we went down and down until we were relegated.

I often reflect sadly on those days and wonder if the present financial plight of Portsmouth could be traced back to then. Of course, a lot of water has flowed under the bridge since, but I still love the club and hope that better days lie ahead.

I had my own battle with Freddie Cox, which came to a head over the Christmas/New year period in 1958, when we were beaten in successive matches, 6 – 0 at West Ham, 5 – 3 at home to Wolves, then the following day 7 – 0 at Molineux. Whilst it was obvious something would have to give after a run of results like that, I didn't feel I played too badly. This was reflected in a review article by 'Linesman' of the *Portsmouth News*:

The Press have not been seeing eye to eye on everything at Fratton Park this season. But here was one time the sports journalists were unanimous. They all agreed that Uprichard was not to blame for the shattering defeats that had embedded Portsmouth at the bottom of the table. I have been looking back at what I wrote about Uprichard after Pompey's 7 – 0 thrashing at Wolverhampton. It looks pretty black for a goalkeeper who lets in 18 goals in three matches. But Uprichard must have the sympathy of everyone who has seen him in action recently. His Boxing Day display at Fratton Park was as good as anything I have seen from a goalkeeper this season. At West Ham, when six goals went past him and at Wolverhampton on Saturday he brought off some brilliant saves. Just what the goals against would have been without the fighting Irishman I shudder to think … I would be the last person to say he was blameless, how many at Fratton Park are blameless? No one can deny he was the most overworked goalkeeper in the League. Even the full backs were coming through to have shots on goal in the match at Wolverhampton when the rest of the defence caved in.

Note the discord between Cox and the press at that stage. I was dropped for the Nottingham Forest match on 3 January 1959, together with three other internationals: left-back Alex Wilson, left-half Tommy Casey and Derek Dougan. Fred Brown, who had signed in the close season from West Brom, took my place but the team again lost 1 – 0.

It was clear the team spirit built up over a number of years by Eddie Lever had been destroyed. I believe some of the most experienced players were dropped to teach us a lesson, rather than improve performance on the pitch. Jimmy Dickinson and Peter Harris, legends at Pompey, did not escape being threatened with being dropped either. Our supporters were very annoyed about what was going on at the club and attendances rapidly started to fall. I was heartened by a fan's letter to the *Portsmouth News*. Mr Hennessy, claiming his views represented those of 200 aircraft machinists in Portsmouth, wrote, 'Uprichard ranks as the finest goalkeeper that Pompey have ever had. At present, although not good enough for Mr. Cox's team, he is keeping Harry Gregg out of the Ireland team. Not to be included is an insult to the player.'

Three days later I felt the time had come when I needed to make a public personal statement, both in my own interests and that of the club. I was well aware the reaction of Mr Cox and the board, who still had confidence in him (or at least publicly), was likely to be vicious. I was warned about this but made my statement to the *Daily Express* on 12 January. It appeared the following day headlined, 'I am a scapegoat, says Uprichard. They're treating me unfairly, complains Portsmouth keeper.'

The statement was:

Ever since I was dropped from the team to play Nottingham Forest, scores of people in and around Portsmouth have stopped me to ask why. Well now I can tell them. The previous Wednesday Mr Freddie Cox called a meeting of the playing staff and he stated that if and when any member of his first eleven was dropped he would send for him and tell him the reason why. On Friday 2 January the team sheet went up as usual and I found my name was missing as well as those of Tom Casey, Derek Dougan and Alex Wilson, all internationals. All of us had played the previous week at Wolverhampton. I waited around at the ground to be sent for and given reasons for my omission. I did not see Cox until the Saturday night (3 Jan) when I returned from Nottingham after playing for the reserves. He was waiting at the station to take me to hospital after I had fractured my knuckle bone again about fifteen minutes after the start of the game. Again he did not say anything regarding my being dropped from the first team.

On the Monday morning he still had not sent for me, so I decided to go and see him. He was free in his office and we had a lengthy discussion. He said his reason for leaving me out was that I had been playing badly. I was dumbfounded as I thought I had been playing quite well, so did almost everyone else on the playing staff and so did the sportswriters.

The club has always been very good to me. I have no grumbles against club, directors or players. But I am positive that I was made scapegoat after the recent run of defeats and I feel I have been treated very unfairly. Of course if another club made an offer for me I should have to give it deep consideration for I am not at all happy with the present situation which finds me dropped from the first team, losing wages, having a broken hand and with my position in the Ireland team jeopardised.

I for one would not like to see the club take the dreary drop to Division Two. After all I've been here six and a half years and I can vouch that every player takes a great pride in the club. I still have good reason to believe a lot of them are not at all happy under the present Cox regime.

I suppose it was quite unusual for a player to make a statement to the press in those days, but I felt so strongly about the issue. It was said straight from the heart without any help and I felt it was the right thing to do. I'm proud I had the guts to do it and I don't regret it in the slightest. If the then board and manager didn't like it, that was their concern. The supporters certainly didn't approve of their behaviour. The club's viciousness towards me and appalling treatment of other experienced first team players had the inevitable disastrous consequences.

The anticipated tantrum from Cox came the day after the article when he told me I would train alone in the afternoon. He advised the press, 'I have told Uprichard I don't want him at the ground in the morning with the rest of the players, he can work by himself in the afternoons and as far as I am concerned, it will stay that way.' The board continued to support Cox and there were some pretty evasive and biting comments made by the chairman Mr Sparshatt in the local press. 'The directors wish it to be made known that the loyalty displayed by nearly every member of the playing staff is appreciated to the full.'

This was contradicted by 'Linesman' on 14 January 1959:

I imagine that the paragraph which caused most annoyance in the Uprichard disclosures was that he had reason to believe that a lot of players were not at all happy under the Cox regime. What are the facts about this? As I know them there are five unhappy men. There is Uprichard ... Then there is the case of Phil Gunter, who also attacked his manager nationally and won his first team place back the following Saturday. His transfer plea was rejected. The latest player wanting to leave is John Phillips, who tells me his transfer request was granted at last week's Board meeting. This has since been denied by the club. Irish international Derek

Dougan expressed his wish to get away but was given a firm "No". The fifth player is Cyril Rutter, on the transfer list at his request. He is the reserve team captain and centre-half. Two other players, Sammy Chapman and Derek Weddle were told the club was willing to receive offers for them. Now Chapman is in the first team.

The debate rumbled on in the national newspapers. On 22 January, Desmond Hackett, one of Fleet Street's finest sports journalists, wrote,

Drop this ban on Uprichard. Portsmouth soccer customers have handed me one of the biggest ever postbags demanding that the club should end its decision to send Norman Uprichard to Coventry and condemn him to train alone. Uprichard got himself into trouble because he wrote in the *Daily Express* that he was not getting a fair deal from the club. Now let's be quite fair about this. No club would be amused by that kind of frank talk and who can blame Portsmouth if they consider that the player be disciplined? But surely when dealing with grown-ups like Uprichard, who has been around Portsmouth since 1952, there are less harsh systems than banishing a man from his fellow players. It appears that this cold shoulder treatment will continue. If it does then it is up to the Football Players' Union to defend this man.

Instead he played in the reserve side against Nottingham Forest. No sulking quitter this man Uprichard. He fractured his hand in action after fifteen minutes and moved to the right wing after a short period for treatment in the dressing room. Even there he became Pompey's hero by scoring the winning goal four minutes from the end.

I remember that reserve match well. The inside right came through with the ball and of course, me being the daredevil I was, I dived at his feet. I got the ball, bang, and it broke the knuckle again in the same place as before. I got it dressed up and went on the wing. From being 2 – 0 down at half-time we made a terrific comeback and I scored the winning goal after Armstrong, their keeper, failed to hold a shot from Brian Naysmith. Of course I was out again for a month – it hadn't exactly been a good week!

When in the first team my wages were £20 per week plus bonus, but when I was in the reserves, they dropped to £17 plus bonus. As I was injured I knew my wages would stick at £17, which was a big drop in those days. I knew it might be some time before I could re-establish myself in the first team. When I pointed this out to Cox he said, 'All you want is to get as much out of the game as you can.' 'Who doesn't,' I replied. 'When I go on the field I give all I have got for my club or country, whichever the case may be. Quite naturally I think I'm entitled to get as much out of the game as I can if I'm putting all I can into it.' I don't think he liked me, and I don't know why. Even at Arsenal we were never friendly. I remember once paying for one of his stupid fines with a bag of pennies, which I threw on his desk.

Things got so bad during Cox's reign, it was brought to my attention, that I was being spied on to see what time I came in at night. Facing the clubhouse where we lived on the corner of Carisbrooke Road and Milton Lane was a row of trees and it was possible to hide behind them. I remember the first time I saw someone was when I went upstairs to get ready for bed and saw this head pop round the first tree in the avenue. I must confess I was in the habit of coming in at 11.30 p.m. or midnight after a night out at the pub, and so decided to devise a method to get over this problem. My house backed right onto Fratton Park and I could see one of the goals out of my back window. Instead of coming through the front door, I used to walk round to the back of the ground, over the gate, along the terracing and over the wall to my back garden. I'm sure one of the trainers was watching me at Cox's instigation, but I was never confronted about it.

All I could do at Fratton Park during my winter of discontent was keep fit. It was very difficult as a goalkeeper to train on my own, as you are more reliant than any other position on your team mates to put in crosses, shots, etc., but I had said my piece and waited to see what happened next. There were, of course, no specialist goalkeeping coaches, not that I have any time for coaches. In my eyes if you can play football you can play in eleven positions. Training and set pieces yes, but I never had anybody coaching me in my whole career. It is either born in you or it is not there.

When my hand injury mended, I went back to serious training in early February, on a normal basis. Cox had cooled down by then, mainly, I think, because of the unprecedented antagonism his making me train alone had caused among the supporters.

My first game after the four week lay-off was for the reserves against Tottenham. Tom Casey and Derek Dougan were also in the side, as was Danny Blanchflower for Spurs. I did get back into the first team eventually, but only for two games. I played in a 1 – 1 home draw with Birmingham City on 21 March 1959, then my last first team game was on Good Friday when we were beaten 6 – 1 by Manchester United at Old Trafford in front of 51,000. Pompey hadn't won a game since November and we slid out of the First Division with a wretched return of twenty-one points. I managed twenty-six games, mainly in the first half of the season. There was still the odd game that stands out. In September 1958, Peter Harris put on a world class show under lights at Fratton Park against Aston Villa, netting all five goals in a 5 – 2 triumph. At the end of the game I ran half the length of the field to congratulate him. As I shook his hand he said, 'Oh away, I should be shot, I missed three sitters.' He was the first winger to score five goals in the First Division and was admonishing himself for having missed a couple of chances – typical.

At the end of the season I was placed on the transfer list by Cox. Tom Casey had already joined Peter Doherty at Bristol City. I'd made 182 league appearances and 13 in the cup and, apart from my run-in with Cox, had thoroughly enjoyed my seven seasons there. The fans were brilliant, as I lived by the ground I often had kids knock on my door asking for autographs and was happy to oblige. However, the manner of my departure left me with mixed emotions, some bitterness and disillusionment, but also much sadness and nostalgia.

During my time at Pompey the biggest pleasure I had was going back to Highbury in October 1954, and beating the Arsenal 1 – 0 with a Peter Harris goal. Tom Whittaker shook my hand and said, 'Well done.' However, it was clear I had no future at Portsmouth and I had to move on.

Chapter Eight

Northern Ireland Memories

Peter Doherty became the Irish international manager in 1951, a post he held for eleven years. I had a huge amount of respect for him and to me he was an incomparable genius on the football field. Those sentiments are shared by Joe Mercer, who regarded him as the greatest player he ever saw. 'Of all the opponents I faced I particularly remember Doherty, who was unplayable on his day. He was built like a greyhound, very fast and elusive but with stamina, too. He had a Rolls-Royce engine in him,' enthused Mercer.

Bill Shankly was quoted as saying, 'Top of them all I would place Peter Doherty. He always gave me the greatest trouble, he was perpetual motion. You could dog, challenge and even hurt him, but you wouldn't dismay him, he kept coming.'

Billy Wright also rated him as one of the outstanding, inside forwards in the world.

So it was a huge thrill for me to know he had been appointed manager and that I might be playing for him sooner rather than later. Before they appointed Peter, I am told the team used to meet a couple of hours before the match, play at Windsor Park, and then disperse. Peter adopted a more professional approach and persuaded the Irish Football Association to bring the team together at least three days before a game, staying at Belfast or Coleraine with proper training facilities.

The 1951–52 season was memorable for me as on 7 October 1951, I made my Northern Ireland debut at Belfast in a 3 – 0 defeat by Scotland, which was Peter's first match as manager. Ted Hinton, who had also competed in the 1940s with Billy Smyth for the goalkeeping position at Distillery, was the existing Irish keeper. I had been having decent press for a while when two Irish selectors were sent to watch me in the Swindon game against Watford in September 1951. I didn't know they were present and only learned of my selection in one of the evening papers the following week, as one did in those days. The Saturday before

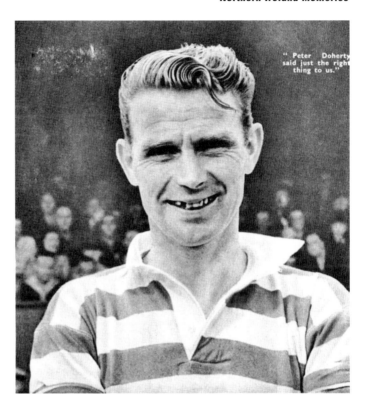
"Peter Doherty said just the right thing to us."

Northern Ireland manager Peter Doherty, a great inspiration to all who played under him.

my debut I had a good game against Walsall and congratulations and good luck were broadcast over the tannoy system from the directors and players of Walsall. That was typical of the friendliness and sportsmanship of that Midlands club and, as we walked off the pitch, big Liam O'Neill, Walsall's inside forward from Belfast Celtic said to me, 'Norman, if you play like that next Saturday you'll be there twenty years.' To give me further confidence Walsall's chairman Neville Longmore told the press, 'It was the best goalkeeping exhibition on the ground since the days of Bert Williams.' Mr Castle, the chairman of Swindon, presented me with a silver cigarette case, which I still have, to commemorate the occasion. To crown it all, Tom Whittaker, with characteristic kindness, sent me a telegram of congratulations and good wishes on hearing of my selection. My friends, Billy Bingham (Sunderland), Jimmy McIlroy (Burnley) and Bertie Peacock (Glasgow Celtic) also made their international debut on that day.

Although I conceded three goals, I think I played pretty well and was walking on air as we left the field at Windsor Park. A report endorsed my feelings:

Cause for satisfaction was the extremely confident first appearance of twenty-three year-old Norman Uprichard. I feel that he is here to stay. From the first minute

Mr Castle, chairman of Swindon Town, presents me with a silver cigarette case to commemorate my first cap for Northern Ireland in October 1951.

I take the field for my first cap, with the Northern Ireland team led by Jack Vernon at Windsor Park in October 1951 against Scotland.

when he caught an awkward ball and came coolly through three bustling Scots, he gave many examples of his capabilities. Under the careful handling of Swindon manager Louis Page, the boy has played himself into Ireland's side and earned the first of what will be, I feel, a series of caps.

The Belfast press were likewise complimentary, with *The Northern Whig* leading, 'Uprichard has come to stay. At last we have a goalkeeper who can hold the ball. Everything he did he did with an assurance which suggests the selectors will have no more worries as far as this department is concerned.' The *Belfast Telegraph* people elected me 'Sportsman of the Weekend' and reported, 'Most encouraging feature was that at last Ireland has found a goalkeeper. Right from the kick-off Uprichard impressed me as confident. Never did he show a symptom of nerves. Always he appeared to make up his mind what he intended to do – and did it. He could not be blamed for any of the goals.'

My other memories were the experience of our captain, Jack Vernon, who at his peak was the best centre half in Britain, to protect me, supported by Alfie McMichael, who learned his trade at Linfield before moving to Newcastle, where he missed out on a FA Cup winner's medal due to injury. Alfie soon became recognised as one of the best left backs in English football and was destined to take over from Jack as captain of the national side. There were solid debuts for Billy Bingham and Bertie Peacock, whilst Jimmy McIlroy had a very rare off day; perhaps the nerves got the better of him. 'Cheeky' Charlie Tully, also known as 'The Lemon Drop Kid', struggled as well, apart from the first ten minutes when he waltzed round George Young at will. Charlie could be brilliant one day and anonymous the next. He liked to 'showboat' at times, but no left winger could mess about for long with big George Young, one of the finest defenders Scotland has produced, and a gentleman. Bobby Johnstone scored two of Scotland's goals, one just before half-time, which was a killer. It was a relatively inexperienced side, compared with the Scots, and Peter Doherty had little time to do much more than instil enthusiasm and hope in our hearts. We didn't realise at the time how he would change the face of Irish football, gradually blooding new, young talent and, with his softly spoken voice, offering shrewd tactical advice culminating in the 1958 World Cup.

The teams were:

Ireland: Uprichard, Graham, McMichael, Dickson, Vernon, Ferris, Bingham, McIlroy, McMorran, Peacock, Tully.
Scotland: Cowan, Young, Cox, Evans, Woodburn, Redpath, Waddell, Johnstone, Reilly, Orr, Liddell.

A presentation of a wireless from the people of Lurgan in recognition of my first senior international cap. Also in the photo are Alf McMichael, Danny Blanchflower, Gerry Morgan, Jimmy D'Arcy, Eddie McMorran, Lily and Peter Doherty.

My second international was against England at Villa Park on 14 November 1951. I was reported as having given a 'wonderful' performance until about seven minutes from time when I managed to clutch a shot just under the crossbar, but somehow it slipped from my grasp to leave Nat Lofthouse with the simple task of tapping it into an empty net. Nat scored both goals that day; he didn't miss many chances or even half chances. I was furious with myself for making that awful mistake because our defence had given a great display up to then and we were still in with a fighting chance of equalising. The general verdict of the press was complimentary, one writer wrote, 'England's much vaunted attack was torn to pieces at times by a tremendous Irish defence. Vernon was at his best and gave the impression that he has still several internationals in front of him.' It was not to be, as Jack's performance proved to be his international swan song. The entire defence covered me brilliantly that day, which is why I had nightmares for some time after about the way I conceded the second goal. In the dressing room Alfie McMichael said to me, 'Don't worry too much Norman, the man who never made a mistake never made anything,' which helped. Equally, there was

Above: The Northern Ireland team that faced England in my second international at Villa Park in November 1951. Back row: Gerry Morgan (trainer), Bill Dickson, Len Graham, myself, Sammy Smyth, Alf McMichael, Danny Blanchflower (twelfth man). Front row: Billy Bingham, Eddie McMorran, Jack Vernon, Frank McCourt, Jimmy McIlroy, John McKenna.

Right: Action from the England game. I clutch a dangerous centre as Nat Lofthouse rises to challenge. Jack Vernon is on the left in his last international.

A point blank save from Jackie Sewell.

An aerial duel with Nat Lofthouse.

sympathy for Sammy Smyth, who early on from 6 yards, with just Gil Merrick to beat, turned the ball over the bar after a beautiful pass from Jimmy McIlroy. Had Sammy and I not made those mistakes, the result would have been a fairer reflection of the game.

Our final international that season was away to Wales on 19 March 1952. We were well on top in atrocious conditions at the Vetch Field when, after about ten minutes of the second half, the Welsh goalkeeper, Bill Short, cleared his lines with a long upfield kick. Trevor Ford, typically, chased the skidding ball when Bill Dickson made a perfectly timed sliding tackle and both fell heavily on the treacherous surface. Immediately, referee Arthur Ellis pointed to the spot. We protested that, if it was a foul, it was committed at least two yards outside the box, but to no avail. Ford, who had been lying prostrate on the ground, made a miraculous recovery as Wally Barnes banged the ball in off my foot. Up to then Bill Dickson had Ford in his pocket, but the manner of the goal took the stuffing out of us and we conceded two goals in the last six minutes to give Wales victory by a score-line that did scant justice to the manner of our performance. As Roy Peskett, a celebrated journalist of the day, put it,

> The Wales forward line, with Ford and Allchurch strangely ineffective, never got together. Northern Ireland, rated as the chopping blocks in this game, put up a surprisingly resolute display. They were extremely unlucky in the period immediately after half-time. It was then that from a Bingham cross, McMorran's flying header hit the upright. A few minutes later McIlroy pivoted and, with the Welsh defence going the wrong way, hit a great shot across and just inches wide of the far side of the goal. McMichael, Dickson, McMorran and Uprichard were the Irish stars.

Those last words gave me a lot of confidence for the future. In the absence of Vernon, Alfie McMichael captained the side for the first time and impressed in that role, as he was to in many future internationals. Dickson was moved to centre half and Danny Blanchflower returned to the international scene at right half. Jimmy D'Arcy replaced Bertie Peacock at inside right.

I was selected for all the Home Internationals of the 1952–53 season and also the France game. Our first encounter was against England at Windsor Park on 4 October 1952. Willie Cunningham and Charlie Tully were back in the fold after a period of international wilderness and with a star-studded side, England were lucky to draw. We were leading 2 – 1 with three minutes to go and the Windsor Park crowd roaring us on when that fine centre half, Jack Froggatt, who became one of my team mates in domestic football, appeared from nowhere on the right wing. He collected a long pass from Billy Wright and cracked over a beautiful out swinger on to the head of Billy Elliott, who coolly nodded it past

Relaxing at Bangor before the international against England in October 1952. From left: Billy Bingham, Willie Cunningham, myself and Billy Neill, who was a reserve.

me. There was really nothing I could do, as the ball was swinging away from me I didn't think it possible to come off my line. Wright had again split our defence, as he did after two minutes, to lay on another goal for Nat Lofthouse. It was a hard-tackling game played in the right spirit. Tom Finney displayed his terrific skill in the opening skirmishes, but Alfie McMichael soon had him under control. Charlie Tully scored both our goals, one direct from a corner that deceived Gil Merrick and the second a beautifully struck volley a minute after half-time. Charlie showed he could be as good a player as Finney when he put his mind to it and didn't over indulge in his 'ball-juggling' act. He gave Alf Ramsey the runaround that day. It gave me personal satisfaction that Harry Ditton wrote,

> The spirit of the Irish side was epitomised by Uprichard who, when he went down in a collision with Lofthouse, would have been justified in having a spell in the dressing room. Indeed that's where the trainers tried to drag him. He not only refused to go but, when they tried to remove his jersey so that one of his colleagues could, temporarily at least, deputise in goal, he obstinately refused to give it up.

In fact it was Billy Elliott who clattered into me. The ambulance men wanted me to go off, but I refused. Eddie McMorran would also have been justified if he had called it a day after an ugly eye injury he received in a clash with Jimmy Dickinson resulted in him being carried off on a stretcher. Eddie was a former Larne blacksmith, a hard man, and trotted back with a bandage on his head to add his weight to the fray. As Ditton remarked, 'It was the spirit of Uprichard and McMorran which inspired the Irish boys to unbelievable endeavour and shook England to the core.' We had not beaten England since 1927, a game our trainer Gerry Morgan played in, but were close to repeating that feat on that day.

We were certainly gaining in confidence under the astute stewardship of Peter Doherty, and starting to blend well as a unit. Scotland was next up at Windsor Park on 5 November 1952. I have always loved bands, flute, accordion or pipe. About an hour before the match I heard the Glasgow Police Pipe Band tuning up and couldn't stop myself from following them round the pitch. With about twenty minutes to go Peter Doherty suddenly realised his goalkeeper wasn't in the dressing room and rushed out to drag me in. I was enjoying myself so much!

The game took place under rain-lashed conditions, but we showed the Scots we had as much staying power as they had. Eventually, after about eighty minutes of deadlock, Jimmy D'Arcy gave us the lead from a pass laid on by Jimmy McIlroy. They put us under a lot of pressure and I made a couple of good saves from George Aitken and Billy Liddell. Then, with just thirty seconds to go, and our supporters at full throttle singing, 'When Irish Eyes are Smiling', victory was snatched from us, just as it had been a month earlier by England. Scotland won a corner taken by Tommy Wright. Charlie Tully was only able to partly clear it to George Young, who lobbed the ball into the penalty area, where centre-forward Lawrie Reilly rose above everybody else to head goalwards. I had it covered, but, through no fault of his, it cruelly glanced off Bill Dickson's head into the net.

The selectors must have been pleased with our overall performance, as minutes after the end they announced practically the same team for the French international. The only change was Peacock coming in for McIlroy, who Burnley initially refused to release, then later relented. On the way back to Swindon I called in at Highbury with two of the Scottish team, Jimmy Logie and Jimmy Scoular, for a spot of training. Little did I realise that before the week was out I would be a club mate of Scoular. Within an incredibly hectic short period of time I was transferred to Portsmouth, the day after the Scotland match, then played for the first time against a continental side.

One of the conditions of my transfer to Portsmouth was that I would be released for the France friendly international in Paris three days after my

POOR CROWD SEE RAIN-LASHED INTERNATIONAL

Last-kick goal robs Ireland of
5ᵗʰ Nov. 1952
dramatic Glasgow win

UPRICHARD HERO OF THE DAY

SCOTLAND 1 (Reilly), IRELAND 1 (D'Arcy).

THIS WAS WINDSOR PARK ALL OVER AGAIN! With only seconds to go—there was no time even to re-centre the ball—Scotland equalised with a holy goal nine minutes after D'Arcy had given Ireland the lead. What a finish! What drama!

The
HAMPDEN
Story

NORMAN UPRICHARD.
A hero.

Above and below: Full stretch to save from George Aitken during the 1 – 1 draw with Scotland at Windsor Park in November 1952.

A fine save by Uprichard, Irish goalkeeper, from a shot by Aitken.

Pompey debut. It was one of the most bizarre matches I ever played in my entire career. We lost the game 3 – 1 but, to be fair, France were much faster to the ball and more skilful. They produced some wonderful ball control and passing movements, tackled hard and generally possessed more know how than us. On the right wing they had twenty-one-year-old Raymond Kopa, who of course became a legend at Real Madrid. What didn't help either is that we didn't have Peter Doherty with us, although I'm not sure why. The team was looked after by a couple of selectors and Gerry Morgan.

What made the game so unusual was that there were twelve French players on the field when they scored their first goal. Centre-forward Cisowski was injured in a tackle, went off and substitute Jean Baratte came on. Shortly after, Cisowski returned. But at that moment right half Bonifaci pulled a muscle, so Baratte stayed on and Cisowski went to outside right. Bonifaci must have been unaware of what happened, because after treatment he came back, thus giving France twelve men! The ball came out to him, he evaded a tackle from our skipper Alf McMichael, swung the ball into the middle and their inside left Ujlaki opened the scoring. Danny Blanchflower led the protests to the referee. We held up our fingers to count and pointed to Bonifaci, who by this time was hobbling off the pitch and down the tunnel. Clearly, the Dutch referee Mr Schipper failed to notice it and after the match admitted to Harry Cavan of the IFA that he had made a mistake in not counting the players. To compound the error he also told him he thought their second goal was offside, but the linesman failed to raise his flag. As the *Belfast Telegraph* headlined, 'Referee thought goal offside but linesman did not signal … Admits he failed to count Frenchmen!' It was altogether a strange game as they struggled to finish as we did, which the *Belfast Telegraph* acknowledged,

Never have I seen an Irish attack so subdued, so completely knocked off its game. It lacked punch, progressive ideas, everything. Only Eddie McMorran came out of it with any credit. While the defence must line up for the bouquets, there was something sluggish about the whole Irish team. There did not seem to be the same enthusiasm, incentive and planned purpose as was evident in the previous internationals this season. The highly efficient pre-match and half-time talks of Peter Doherty, the team manager, were missing. Long before the interval it was obvious that things were not working well up front. And that is where Doherty would have excelled … Head and shoulders above everyone else was that hero of Hampden, Norman Uprichard. Before the game he confessed he was nervous, playing for the first time against continentals. But here we had a flashback to the halcyon days of the great Elisha Scott.

Beaten by a strike from Raymond Kopa (right) for the second goal in the 3 – 1 defeat to France at Paris in November 1952. Bill Dickson (No. 5) desperately tries to keep the shot out.

To be compared with Scott, who played with such distinction for Liverpool and Northern Ireland in the 1920s and 1930s, was very flattering.

After the game the French made amends by entertaining us to a lavish dinner with unlimited cocktails, wine and liqueurs. We got absolutely pissed, and after the dinner my pal Charlie Tully and I went out on the town until we ran out of money. We staggered back to the hotel and asked the secretary if we could have an advance of our match fee. He let us have part of it and we carried on drinking until about 4.30 a.m., when we fancied some fish and chips. We rolled up at this restaurant and the owner, pointing at this huge fish tank, asked us what we wanted. We chose these huge fish, which he cooked and we polished them off with chips and made our way back to the hotel in time for breakfast!

Above: The Ireland Football Association party about to board the *Empress of Scotland* for the 1953 tour of USA and Canada.

Next page: On board the *Empress of Scotland*. Back row: myself, Norman Lockhart, Tommy Casey, Len Graham, John Scott, Danny Blanchflower, Eddie McMorran, Sammy Hughes, Bruce Shiels, Alf McMichael, Gerry Morgan, Jimmy McCabe. Front row: Gerry Bowler, Frank McCourt, Billy Drennan (secretary), A. Kennedy, Fred Cochrane (president), S. Walker, Ray Ferris, Billy Neill, Eddie Crossan, Jimmy D'Arcy.

We came up against the mighty John Charles in the home international against Wales on 15 April 1953. Although we only lost 3 – 2, it was not a strong performance from us, reflected in Ralph the Rover's report in the *Belfast Newsletter*:

> Those much cherished hopes of Ireland sharing the International championship have gone … from goal outwards Ireland were a bunch of ineffective units who switched, turned and twisted in unavailing efforts to bring some co-ordination … Wales won this match because they had balance in every department.

Eddie McMorran, who scored both our goals, and Charlie Tully were about our only players who came out of the game with any credit and John Charles, who also scored twice, was the best player on the pitch. Charles was the best centre-forward I played against – he was never dirty. A lot of forwards hit me – Trevor Ford, Lofthouse, etc. – but Charles didn't need to, he was so clever. He lived up to his 'Gentle Giant' nickname and was a very nice man.

The 1952–53 season had seen me break through to the First Division and retain my place as Ireland's number one keeper. It was with much anticipation that the Irish Football Association organised a summer tour of Canada. After all, a bunch of young Irish footballers travelling abroad was the perfect opportunity to let our hair down after a long season. There were twenty of us in all, including selectors and administrators, for an eleven game tour of USA and Canada. The majority of players were full internationals, but also included were two good Irish League players, Sammy Hughes of Glentoran and Bruce Shiels of Cliftonville. The luxurious *Express of Scotland* sailed from Belfast to Liverpool in early May 1953, then from Liverpool the following day to Montreal. We arrived in Montreal and travelled down to New York by train a week or so later, where we played Liverpool on 14 May at Ebbets Field, which was baseball club Brooklyn Dodgers ground. After all the luxury travelling, although we had a training session every day aboard the *Express*, we were far from match sharp and they beat us 4 – 0, with a brace each from Billy Liddell and Louis Bimpson. In truth, because of the wonderful kindness and hospitality we received throughout that tour, we were never fully fit. However, our primary aim was to foster interest in the game in those parts.

After our defeat we spent four days sightseeing in New York. One day we were walking past Jack Dempsey's restaurant at Times Square. I was trailing behind everybody as we passed a couple of guys leaning on the railings and one of them said, 'Excuse me bud, are you guys the Irish soccer stars?' I said, 'Yes.' 'Are you the Irish soccer coach?' to which I replied, 'No sir I'm the slow coach!'

One morning I went into a supermarket to buy some presents for Lily and her mother. Nylons were the rage then, but not so easy to buy in Ireland. Whilst waiting to pay for them, three of my team mates were deep in conversation with a store detective at the exit. Just then a lightning strike occurred in the store for reasons I will never know. I asked the girl at the counter, who was just leaving, what to do with my purchase. 'Please yourself, I'm on strike,' she replied casually. So I approached the detective, he was still talking to my mates, who discovered he had been born near Ballymena and was reminiscing with them. He said, 'Because of the strike I can't take money off you and, from what these guys have told me about you, I don't think anybody could take the nylons off you either.' I wasn't quite sure what he meant but, judging from the chuckles from the other players, they had clearly been spinning him a yarn or two. 'Take them with you, it's not your fault they won't let you pay for them, I'll sort it out later,' he continued. I was well pleased with my bargain that day. Shortly after, we entered a bar off Broadway to have a meal and a few drinks. We were in our uniform of green jackets, grey trousers, etc. I ordered four bottles of Guinness which at $1.50 per bottle was quite pricey, especially as the four of us only had about $30 between us by this time. As I was about to pay a guy came over and enquired who we were. When we explained he said he was Irish himself and told us if we could gather up the rest of party to sign a gigantic menu he produced, we could eat and drink free of charge for the rest of the evening. It didn't take much persuasion for the rest of the lads to be rounded up and join us and, needless to say, I don't remember much of that evening!

From there we played at Hamilton, Ontario, where we beat Hamilton All-Stars 4 – 1. After the game one of the All-Stars team took me out for the evening, showing me the sights of Hamilton and gave me a silver dollar for Lily, which I still have. From Hamilton we moved to Toronto, where there were more Ulstermen than anywhere else in Canada and, needless to say, the party continued. We stayed about four days, had a wonderful time, and beat an Ontario Select side 2 – 0. Three days later we were at the Osborne Stadium, Winnipeg, where goals from Sammy Hughes, who top-scored with ten on the tour, and John Scott saw off the Winnipeg Select XI.

Our next stop was Moose Jaw in Saskatchewan, where we beat the Saskatchewan FA team 10 – 0. Their manager was Gerry Haughey, the former Glenavon outside-right, who confirmed what a difficult job it was at the time to promote the game. The match itself was originally scheduled to take place at the local baseball ground in Moose Jaw, but was waterlogged because of a heavy downpour. It was switched to an improvised pitch out on the prairie where the fun and games began. Both teams travelled to the new venue together and stripped off in a small hotel – all thirty three of us, as Saskatchewan had eleven reserves. Shortly after the start of the match, about two dozen prairie dogs invaded the pitch. It proved impossible to round them up and the ball got a bit of a battering. Afterwards we were made honorary members of the Moose Jaw Irish Society and presented with the colourful badges worn by the Moose Jaw team on their shirts.

From there we went to Lake Louise in the Canadian Rockies to take in a little of their breathtaking scenery, fresh mountain air and consume innumerable barbecued steaks. Some of us persuaded a member of the Royal Canadian Mounted Police to loan Gerry Morgan a uniform in Banff. We got him in it and sent him off on a sightseeing tour in the most colourful garb of his colourful career. 'Mighty fine, mighty fine', was all Gerry could say the entire afternoon.

We then went down the Fraser Valley to Vancouver, capital of British Columbia, where we played twice, winning the first 3 – 1. In between these games we moved to Victoria – beautifully decorated and full of colourful parades for the Queen's Coronation. We beat Victoria Select XI 5 – 1 before returning to Vancouver to play our second game there, which we lost 3 – 2, mainly because of a questionable penalty decision by the referee. Whilst they were the best side we played, apart from Liverpool, it was a bit of an embarrassment to lose against them. They included Fred Whittaker, formerly of Notts County, and Earl Crossan, who later returned to play for Manchester City and Southend, so were no mugs, but we should have beaten them.

The match was actually played on Coronation Day and after the game 'Mrs Football' of Canada, Mrs Richardson, widow of John Richardson, former BC Soccer Commissioner, laid on a party for us, so we didn't need much persuasion to drown our sorrows. We all had a good time, including, of course, yours truly, who got stoned out of his 'dome', but I wasn't the only one. Everything was on the house and three of us – me, Ray Ferris and one other who I can't remember after all these years – were reprimanded for our behaviour. I can't remember actually what I did, but probably had an argument with someone being the rebel I was. Ray actually sustained a bad leg injury on that tour that effectively ended his career. I stayed in bed until lunchtime next day and when I appeared Alfie McMichael gave me an envelope with $200. The boys had a sweep on the Derby and Gordon Richards had won for the first time in his long and distinguished career. I had drawn him in the sweep, so took Alfie and several others out for a pub lunch with some of my winnings.

We then moved away far west to Edmonton, capital of the province of Alberta, where on 8 June we defeated the Alberta FA 9 – 1. I remember Danny Blanchflower captained us for the first time as Alfie McMichael was injured. As the sides took the field one of the Alberta players shouted, 'How are you Norman?' It was wee Bobby Baird from Lurgan – we played together as boys for the school team. Bobby was an excellent left winger and had a very good game that night. Afterwards we had a good chat about our schooldays.

On our return journey we travelled via Canadian Pacific Railways for almost three days before we reached Ontario. We were taken to see the nearby Niagara Falls, and then returned to Toronto to play Liverpool again, who beat us this time 3 – 1. I remember during the game stopping a characteristic rocket from Billy Liddell. The impact didn't break any fingers, but it did loosen all the joints and I knew my injury from the previous season hadn't really cleared up. The Toronto Ulster Club presented us with beautiful white shirts and green ties before we moved on to Montreal, playing our last game of the tour against a Swiss side. They beat us 4 – 1 but we were exhausted even before we took to the field, with the travelling, socialising and high humidity. The nearest we came to scoring was when the ball went in through a hole in the side netting, which the linesman spotted. The referee called for a packing needle and some cord and sewed up the hole while we stood around admiring his skill! We returned to Liverpool on the *Empress of France*. During the voyage we agreed what a wonderful experience the trip had been and, when we went our separate ways, were sad that such a special family had broken up and the party was over. My own reality check came when I found to my dismay that I was a stone heavier than my fighting weight. The inevitable treadmill of pre-season training was just around the corner.

The squad comprised of Len Graham, Jimmy McCabe, Alf McMichael, Danny Blanchflower, Ray Ferris, Gerry Bowler, Billy Neill, Tommy Casey, Frank McCourt, John Scott, Bruce Shiels, Eddie Crossan, Jimmy D'Arcy, Eddie

McMorran, Sammy Hughes, Norman Lockhart and of course myself. Malcolm Brodie also covered the tour for the press. I find it very sad that the other sixteen in the squad have all passed away, so I call myself 'The Last of the Irish Rover', which of course is a traditional Irish song about a sailing ship. I guess there's not many people who can say they played in goal against Liverpool in three different countries in one year.

In my absence, because of the hand injury during the 1953–54 season, Billy Smyth, my old Distillery superior, took over my duties for the internationals against England and Scotland. For the April 1954 game against Wales at Wrexham, Harry Gregg appeared on the scene. Harry was with Doncaster Rovers at the time and played brilliantly as we beat Wales 2 – 1. Peter McParland and Billy McAdams also made their debuts and turned in fine displays. My old Arsenal colleague, Jack Kelsey, gained his first cap in goal for Wales. Harry was playing very well at the time and of course moved to Manchester United. I read about the Munich disaster in a newspaper headline outside a shop in Portsmouth. It was a hell of a shock and it was a while before I knew Harry was ok. Harry is a very great friend; I have always respected him as a goalkeeper and person, and we still keep in touch.

When our first home international against England took place in October 1954 at Windsor Park I was back in between the sticks where I remained as first choice throughout the home international series and the following season as well. I believe I reached my peak during those two seasons, especially the 1955–56 season, both at club and international level. It gave me extra motivation that Harry was breathing down my neck; competition was always healthy for both of us.

We were beaten 2 – 0 by England in what was for me, a disappointing return to the international scene. I accept the blame for the first goal when Johnny Haynes caught me in no-man's land. The old maestro, Stanley Matthews, was still waltzing up the right wing twenty years after his first appearance for England. In fact, he made England's second goal a minute later by snaking through and sending Bill Dickson the wrong way. He released the ball to Johnny Haynes, who found Don Revie and his shot beat me all the way and hit the inside of the post. On another occasion Matthews beat Alfie McMichael to the byline, but I managed to drop on his curling cross. We made the running most of the time, but the second goal knocked the stuffing out of us and we couldn't finish some well crafted moves. Danny Blanchflower, in particular, was prominent in attack and defence. The crowd was upset when I was flattened by Nat Lofthouse – Harry Gregg (from the 1958 FA Cup Final) and I knew he could be over vigorous. He was a good player with a hell of a shot – in fact, he had the hardest shot in football along with Trevor Ford and Derek Dooley. However, I would never rank

International comeback match following my lost season, the 2 – 0 defeat by England at Windsor Park in October 1954. Back row: Danny Blanchflower, Jackie Blanchflower, myself, Bill Dickson, Frank Montgomery. Front row: Jimmy McIlroy, Billy Simpson, Alf McMichael, Billy Bingham, Peter McParland, Bertie Peacock.

him in the same class as Tommy Lawton or Jackie Milburn – as a footballer or a gentleman.

My next home international was against Scotland at Hampden Park in November 1954. A 2 – 2 draw sounds exciting, but in truth the only notable incident was an injury to Danny Blanchflower in the second half, which reduced him to hobbling on the right wing. After seventy-four minutes the ball deflected into the net off one of our defenders, which completely deceived me for their equaliser. Wales were the final opposition in April 1955 at Windsor Park. We were beaten 3 – 2, John Charles scoring a hat-trick, despite being policed well by Ernie McCleary. Danny Blanchflower again performed strongly and Eddie Crossan and Jimmy Walker scored our goals; it was Jimmy's first international appearance.

I feel I reached my international peak during the 1955–56 season, especially in the first match at Windsor Park against Scotland in October 1955. Whilst the results hadn't gone our way the previous season, there was still a feeling that Peter

Fisting away a threatening England attack.

Doherty was shaping a side to be reckoned with. Danny Blanchflower had become a shrewd tactician and one of the best half-backs in the United Kingdom. His brother, Jackie, and Peter McParland had appeared on the scene. Len Graham, Billy Bingham, Bertie Peacock and Jimmy McIlroy were all experienced and established and knew each other's strengths and weaknesses. Willie Cunningham, who had deputised for Alfie McMichael at Hampden the previous year, was earning his fifth cap. Only Terry McCavana, earning his second cap, and Fay Coyle of Coleraine on his international debut, were comparative novices, but that game more than justified Peter Doherty's confidence in them. Both gave impressive performances in what must have seemed for them somewhat strange company.

We beat them 2 – 1 against all the odds – the first time we had done for eight years. We took the Scotland defence apart in the first half, with goals from Jackie Blanchflower, a header, and Billy Bingham, with a close range shot, and Fay Coyle made important contributions to both. Scotland came out with all guns blazing in the second half and I had to be at my best to keep them at

The Northern Ireland team that faced Wales at Windsor Park in April 1955 on my 27th birthday. My 'present' was a 3 – 2 defeat. Back row: Jimmy McIlroy, Len Graham, myself, Alf McMichael, Tom Casey. Front row: Eddie Crossan, Jimmy Walker, Danny Blanchflower, Billy Bingham, Norman Lockhart, Ernie McCleary.

bay. Eventually, on the hour, a mistake by Danny Blanchflower in an otherwise flawless performance let them in for a scrambled goal. Despite intense pressure I managed to thwart every effort from the Scots and we held on for a famous victory. I was thrilled with the efforts of my teammates and when I look back on my career it was the best international performance of my career. I make no apology for repeating some of the newspaper headlines such as, 'It's Uprichard the Great at Windsor', 'He Bars the Way in Hectic Scots Rally' and 'Call this the Uprichard International'. I was elated by the reports.

Henry Jones:

Uprichard the Magnificent. Thousands of happy Irish fans raced across the pitch, dozens of them heading for one man. Up went Norman Uprichard to be carried from the pitch after the Scots had been vanquished. And how right were the fans. No need to tell them who saved Ireland in the second half, which was a heartbreak to the Scots and a nightmare to Ireland.

Rex, a Scottish reporter :

On the final blast of the referee's whistle Scots goalkeeper Tommy Younger hared up field from his goal like he's sat on a hot iron. But the Irish fans at the other end beat him to it. They swarmed onto the pitch and lifted the Irish goalkeeper onto their shoulders. When the burly Younger arrived he had to struggle over the heads of the standard bearers to clutch Uprichard's hand. Tommy was doing what everyone in that crowd would have liked to do. For if goalkeepers have a daft day now and again, the big Portsmouth one went stark raving mad. He so often did the impossible that, so far as the Scots were concerned, the possible automatically became impossible.

The People:

Keeper Uprichard hero of great win over Scotland. Norman was without doubt man of the match. In the last half hour he was magnificent as he stopped everything the Scots could throw at him. His greatest save of all was one from Bobby Johnstone which he grabbed with a backward flip.

The esteemed Irish reporter Malcolm Brodie in *Ireland's Saturday Night*:

Call this the Uprichard International. On today's showing in front of a huge crowd at Windsor Park, Norman Uprichard put himself in front of a line of great Irish goalkeepers. He can be honoured with the Scotts, Elisha and Billy, Tommy Breen and Fred McKee. Could there be any greater tribute than this? He was superb. Indeed superlatives fail us to describe his display in the closing half hour when a Scottish side, hitherto not of much account as attackers, suddenly got new life when they were given the gift of a goal. Shots came at Uprichard from all angles. They tried them on the ground, attempted speculative lobs, had twisting, curling efforts, but Norman was simply not to be beaten. This was HIS day.

To be bracketed by Malcolm Brodie with Elisha Scott, Tommy Breen, who replaced Elisha, and further back in the annals of history, Fred McKee and Billy Scott made me feel very humble. The supporters played their part too, as they hoisted me to their shoulders at the end of the game. Tommy Younger ran from the far end of the park to offer his congratulations and struggled to reach me as I was carried to the dressing room. It's a wonderful memory. I seem to recall, vaguely, we had an epic party at Belfast's Grand Central Hotel afterwards. After all it was the first time I'd tasted victory in an Irish shirt on my eleventh appearance.

One of the highlights of my career, as I repel another Scotland attack in the 2 – 1 victory over Scotland at Windsor Park in October 1955.

Lawrie Reilly rushes in as I turn the ball round the upright during the Scotland win.

THE GOALKEEPERS: HERO AND VANQUISHED

Carried off the Windsor Park pitch by jubilant supporters.

IT'S UPRICHARD THE GREAT

He bars the way in hectic Scots' rally

IRELAND HOLD OUT FOR THRILLING WIN

MATCH

	Ireland	Scotland
Goals	2	1
Goal kicks	15	11
Corners	5	13
Throws-in	44	44
Offsides	3	1
Total stoppages	49	70
Attempts at goal	11	21

Total playing time—62 mins. 51 secs.

FACTS

VISITORS IN GAY AND GENEROUS MOOD

THE PROVERBIAL ... OF THE SCOTS was disproved ... before to-day ... ... of the Scottish football fans. They gave away ... ... to the children who were making the customary plea of: "Lift us over, mister."

Other Scots arriving by bus showered pennies out of the windows to children standing around.

About 20 youngsters got in free, thanks to the generosity of these football fans.

One or two boys showed promising "spiv-sense" by trying to re-sell their free tickets, but they could find no buyers.

Although it was October many of the crowd complained of being too warm—there was a mild warm wind blowing from the Cave Hill.

Then came the Scots, with the giant George Young at the head.

After the National Anthem the teams were presented to the Governor, Lord Wakehurst, who was accompanied by officials of both the Irish and Scottish Football Associations.

Before the kick-off, a minute's silence was observed in memory of Mr. R. W. Seeldrayers, president of the Federation de Internationale Football Associations, who died in Brussels yesterday.

Both teams wore black armbands ... ... were flown ...

IRELAND 2. SCOTLAND 1

(J. BLANCHFLOWER, BINGHAM)   (J. ONSTONE)

CALL THIS THE UPRICHARD INTERNATIONAL. AT WINDSOR PARK, WHERE A HUGE CROWD NORMAN UPRICHARD, THE PORTSMOUTH 'KEEP LINE OF GREAT IRISH GOALKEEPERS. HE CA SCOTTS, TOMMY BREEN AND FRED McKEE. COUL TRIBUTE THAN THIS?

He was superb. Indeed, superlatives fail us to d closing half-hour, when a Scottish side, hitherto not c suddenly got new life when they were given the "c Uprichard from all angles. They tried them on the tive lobs, had twisting, curling efforts—but Norman v This was HIS day.

Was this victory deserved? Taking it over all, the answer is decidedly yes. For the first five minutes there was an almost helpless air about the Irish side. Visions loomed of yet another dismal defeat. Passes went astray, and there was a complete lack of confidence and poise in defence.

ON TO-DAY'S SHOWING AW AN IRISH VICTORY, PUT HIMSELF IN THE HONOURED WITH THE HERE BE ANY GREATER

cribe his display in the uch account as attackers, of a goal. Shots came at und, attempted specula- simply not to be beaten.

FULL DESCRIPT

Quick goa

The back page from *Ireland's Saturday Night*, 'It's Uprichard the Great at Windsor Park'.

The teams were:

Ireland: Uprichard, Graham, Cunningham, Blanchflower (D), McCavana, Peacock, Bingham, Blanchflower (J), Coyle, McIlroy, McParland.
Scotland: Younger, Parker, McDonald, Evans, Young, Glen, Smith, Collins, Reilly, Johnstone, Liddell.

After all the euphoria we were brought down to earth in our next international with a 3 – 0 defeat at Wembley against England in November 1955. The only change in the team was the replacement of Jackie Blanchflower at inside left by Charlie Tully. Jackie stayed in the squad as a reserve – after all, he did score our first goal against the Scots, but struggled with the pace of the game, particularly in the second half. It was the first time an Irish team had appeared at Wembley and we all felt honoured to be part of that historic occasion, apart from Gerry Morgan, whose retort was, 'Nonsense, the greyhounds have been running here for fifty years.' It was a new look England side we faced, after they struggled at Cardiff ten days previously. Gone were Bert Williams, Stanley Matthews and Nat Lofthouse. Ron Baynham returned in goal, Ronnie Clayton took over at right half and Bill Perry at outside left for their first caps. Tom Finney switched to the right and Johnny Haynes, Bedford Jezzard and Dennis Wilshaw were back.

Johnny Haynes was undoubtedly the star, as he put Wilshaw through after fifty-one minutes with a trademark diagonal pass behind our full back. I dived for him, but he sidestepped me neatly and steered the ball into an empty net. Three minutes later Perry sent over a superb cross which caught me in no-man's land and Wilshaw nipped in with a back header. Haynes was finding the wide players at will and he swung out a pass to Finney, who hit a shot that I scarcely saw. Fortunately it hit the post but, with three minutes remaining, Finney collected another pass, this time from Jezzard, accelerated past Len Graham and hit a beautiful low shot into the far corner of the net. There's no doubt we had chances to make the scoreline more respectable and didn't disgrace ourselves on the day, particularly in the goalless first half. Billy Bingham swung over a centre which Billy Wright missed and Charlie Tully let fly with a close range shot which Baynham tipped over magnificently. Baynham did misjudge a cross from Peter McParland, which Bingham headed back into the danger area but all to no avail. Coyle pushed the ball towards the empty goal but Jimmy McIlroy tried to help it in and was adjudged offside.

One press report provided an analysis of my performance on this historic occasion:

After inter-passing in midfield Haynes pushed across a pass which Jezzard hit well with his left foot. Fortunately Uprichard had advanced to narrow the angle and

Left: A slightly anxious pose before the start of the Wembley international against England in November 1955.

Below: Presented to the Earl of Derby before start of the England international.

beat the shot out. Later a back heel by Finney gave Jezzard a chance of a first-time shot which was so fast that Uprichard only held it at the second attempt. Finney was having the better of left back Graham, but Uprichard's judgement of his centres was so good that he cut them off before they crossed the goal. Jezzard broke away on the right, cut in and swung a centre to Perry. It looked like a replica of Perry's winning goal in the 1953 cup final as he swung his right foot to it, but Uprichard tipped the fierce shot over the bar.

I dreamed that one day I would play at Wembley, which always had a fascination for me. It all began when, with a crowd of other wee lads, we packed ourselves into a woman's house in Lurgan – she had the only radio in the street – and listened to the commentary of the 1939 Portsmouth *v.* Wolves FA Cup Final. Little did I know then I would become Pompey's goalkeeper.

We concluded our 1955–56 Home International programme with a 1 – 1 draw against Wales at Ninian Park, Cardiff, in April 1956. We had a mediocre first half, but more than compensated by providing a wonderful display after the interval where we completely outplayed the opposition. Although John Charles was this time playing at centre half, he made his presence felt, as he so often did against me, as an attacking force as early as the tenth minute. He dribbled the ball from his own penalty area to just outside the box before releasing Trevor Ford, who let the ball run to Roy Clarke, who opened the scoring. Norman Lockhart raised our hopes when he nipped in between Sherwood and Charles but Jack Kelsey held his centre. Shortly after came a harsh decision against us. When Jackie Blanchflower tackled Ford, he had the misfortune to meet a bouncing ball with his hand as it fell. It was unintentional, but justice was done as I managed to keep out Roy Paul's penalty by diving full stretch to the left. Two minutes after the interval we equalised. Billy Bingham received a pass from Danny Blanchflower and centred for Jimmy Jones to sweep the ball into the net. Soon after I managed to throw myself at the feet of Ford when he was clean through to prevent a certain goal, but we were the dominant force in the second half and Jack Kelsey made a great save when McIlroy put Jones in again. I thwarted Ivor Allchurch at the other end but overall we considered ourselves unfortunate not to win. This was my best game against Wales and of course, the penalty save was a highlight. Jimmy Jones was a big, bustling centre forward, playing in his first international and hit Jack Kelsey, my old Arsenal teammate a few times. As we came off at half-time Jack asked me where we had got him from. I said we picked him up on the boat coming over to make the numbers up!

With the exception of my international swansong against Scotland at Hampden in 1958, the Wales game marked the end of my career as Northern Ireland's first choice keeper. In the 1956–57 season and thereafter, Harry Gregg took over. I

Tipping a dangerous cross from Bill Perry over the bar. Right back Willie Cunningham looks on anxiously.

Saving at the feet of Dennis Wilshaw.

Rising with Danny Blanchflower and Dennis Wilshaw to ward off another England attack.

Intercepting a pass from Johnny Haynes meant for Tom Finney (right).

The Irish team that drew 1 – 1 against Wales in April 1956 at Ninian Park. Back row: Willie Cunningham, Jackie Blanchflower, myself, Alf McMichael, Tommy Casey. Front row: Eddie McMorran, Jimmy McIlroy, Danny Blanchflower, Billy Bingham, Norman Lockhart, Jimmy Jones.

I manage to gather the ball safely from Trevor Ford during the 1 – 1 draw against Wales in April 1956.

Saving a penalty from Roy Paul in the Wales game.

did play in the first international of the 1957–58 season on 5 October against Scotland, but only as Harry's deputy. Harry was still with Doncaster Rovers at the time, as was Peter Doherty. Rovers had made a poor start to the season, were bottom of the Second Division, and Harry couldn't be released to attend. Peter did pay me the compliment of saying I had never let Ireland down in the past which, coming from such a great man, meant a lot to me. It was the first time we had met Scotland without the legendary George Young, who was there in his new capacity of a reporter. The result was goalless, mainly due to the brilliance of my opposite number Tommy Younger. His display was compared with my performance in 1955, as he kept out everything we threw at him. The match was so one-sided I didn't get the opportunity to shine and, with Harry in such great form, I was resigned to playing second fiddle.

In all, I deputised in four internationals: the Scotland game, an Italy play-off game, the World Cup play-off game against Czechoslovakia in Sweden in June 1958 and against Spain in October 1958 at the wonderful Real Madrid Bernabeu Stadium, but more about that later.

Chapter Nine

The Irish Come of Age

The 1958 World Cup Finals, the sixth staging of the World Cup, were hosted by Sweden in June 1958. After a previously unsuccessful attempt to qualify four years earlier, little was expected of our chances upon embarking on the campaign when paired with Portugal and Italy in Group 8. In the event we had to overcome Italy in the final group game, a nation that had never failed to qualify for the finals. The match was originally scheduled at Windsor Park for 4 December 1957, but the Hungarian referee Zsolt was fogbound in London and understandably, the Italian officials would not agree to the employment of a local referee. The game went ahead with Harry in goal as a friendly, much to the annoyance of some of our most excitable Irish supporters. Afterwards, many of them invaded the pitch and the Italian players thought they were going to be lynched. The big centre-half Rino Ferrario became known as the 'Gladiator of Belfast', as he floored about half a dozen fans, some of whom only wanted his autograph! Eventually, the police got the Italians to their dressing room comparatively unscathed. It was all a terrible mix-up which ended happily.

The Italians returned in January 1958, including the big Ferrario, his face wreathed in smiles for the photographers and women admirers he had won at the end of the first game. Before the match we had been training just outside Coleraine on the coast and were on the coach driving to Belfast, which is quite a long way. We stopped at Halls Hotel at Antrim for lunch before the match. Peter Doherty told me at about midday that Harry was fogbound at Manchester, having played for Manchester United the previous night. Peter confirmed that I was playing, just as I was looking forward to a nice big meal. I settled for tea and toast instead, as usual before a game, and went out starving. Peter was an excellent manager. He was quiet, unassuming, and you did what he told you. He related it in a way that you listened and remembered, and got the best out of us. I had been going to watch a match and, not for the first time, ended up playing in it. I must admit to a tightness in my stomach – all Italy had to do was get a draw, but we needed a win.

Lining up for the anthem before the crucial World Cup qualifier against Italy in January 1958. Danny Blanchflower, Willie Cunningham, Jackie Blanchflower, Billy Bingham, myself, Jimmy McIlroy, Bertie Peacock, Wilbur Cush, Billy Simpson, Peter McParland, Alf McMichael.

Once out on the pitch, I fielded a couple of shots early on, which gave me confidence. The nerves disappeared and the adrenaline kicked in. The game was won in the first half, reflected in Malcolm Brodie's comments,

It was a victory richly deserved – a triumph of tactics and teamwork. Ireland was unquestionably the superior football side, both in defence and attack. Peter Doherty's plan to rupture the Italian defensive system worked magnificently. Cush and McIlroy interchanged in bewildering fashion and more havoc was caused by the deep-lying play of Billy Simpson. Norman Uprichard proved himself a capable deputy for Harry Gregg. This was especially so in the first half. He brought off several magnificent saves early on when the Italian forwards looked like doing something ... Bertie Peacock has rarely had a better international. The same could be said of Jackie Blanchflower, who was cool, calm and collected in everything he did ... Ireland's first goal came after fifteen minutes. It was spectacular. Peacock laid it on for McIlroy to beat 'keeper Bugatti all the way from about twenty-five yards out ... A free kick to Italy looked dangerous. With the Irish defence lined up in a solid phalanx Da Costa flighted the ball over their heads and right half Invernizzi was just beaten to the draw by Uprichard. In twenty-nine minutes Ireland were two up. A superb through pass from Danny Blanchflower left Cush on his own. He had time to think where to put the ball. He rammed the first shot hard to the left; Bugatti threw himself full length and made a brilliant save. But the ball ran clear and Cush moved in and hit it first time into the net. After this the Ireland forwards threw everything they had at the Italians who however broke away and a Pivatelli drive was magnificently saved by Uprichard. What a game Norman was having. However Ireland's forwards combined to bewilder the Italian defence, particularly Simpson, who was wandering back. Through his deep-lying policy he began a movement which had the Italian defence at sixes and sevens. McIlroy, Cush and Bingham all took part in the movement ... which ended with McIlroy shooting over the bar.

We went in at half-time leading 2 – 0 to tremendous applause from the crowd and started the second half where we left off. However, in the fifty-seventh minute their outside left, Da Costa, got his toe to the ball from a lob, just as I was stretching full length and had it in my grasp on my goal-line. I fumbled and shouldn't have let him kick it from my hands. It was my fault and unsettled us. The Italians applied more pressure but we came back and Bugatti had to make two magnificent saves from McParland and McIlroy. When the final whistle blew I almost cried with a mixture of joy and relief, as my mistake could have been so much more costly.

Both teams played clean football and this time the crowd behaved very well. Consequently, the Italians were unlucky to have their fine – outside right Ghiggia sent was off for hacking down Alfie McMichael. Alfie protested that Ghiggia had not committed a serious or dirty offence, but referee Zsolt ignored him. Perhaps he didn't understand what Alfie said in his broad Irish brogue, but he must have gathered the gist of it, as Alfie was shaking his head in the way a man says, 'No' and pushed Ghiggia back onto the field. We all felt sorry for him, such was the spirit of the way the game was played in those days.

Back in the dressing room, I embraced Peter Doherty, the architect of the victory, who made sure we worked hard for each other and gave us the confidence and spirit to believe in ourselves. The Italians were understandably distraught, they were on a bonus of £500 each to win or draw. We were paid the usual £50 international fee!

The teams were:

Uprichard fists the ball over the bar during an Italian attack. Jackie Blanchflower (left), Peacock and McMichael (in goal) watch anxiously.

Above: Fisting the ball over the bar during an Italian attack. Jackie Blanchflower (left), Bertie Peacock and Alf McMichael (No. 3) watch anxiously.

Left: Italy's goal as Da Costa gets his toe to the ball as I try to hold it.

VITH **WORLD CHAMPIONSHIP · JULES RIMET CUP 1958**

SWEDEN · SVERIGE

Identity card - Legitimationskort
Player - Spelare

Name: U p r i c h a r d

Christian name: Norman

Country: N.Ireland

FÉDÉRATION INTERNATIONALE
DE FOOTBALL ASSOCIATION
General Secretary

(P.T.O.)

My Identity Card for the World Cup in Sweden. The reverse states 'Free Admission to the Stadium Standing Enclosure'.

Nothern Ireland: Uprichard, Cunningham, McMichael, D. Blanchflower, J. Blanchflower, Peacock, Bingham, Cush, Simpson, McIlroy, McParland.
Italy: Bugatti, Guido, Corradi, Invernizzi, Ferrario, Segato, Ghiggia, Schiaffino, Pivatelli, Montuori, Da Costa.

Belfast went wild that night and so did I. The Italian fraternity in Belfast was going to meet up with the Italian side for a big party at a hotel, as they thought they would beat us. Jackie Blanchflower and I found our way there and got high as kites. At the end of the night we caught a taxi back into the centre of Belfast to our hotel where, at 5.30 in the morning, we were enjoying another nightcap.

The World Cup finals were notable for marking the debut on the world stage of a then largely unknown seventeen-year-old Pele. For Northern Ireland it was the culmination of six years hard work and endeavour by Peter Doherty. The other three home countries also qualified, leaving a strong British representation.

There were only seventeen players in the party that flew to Sweden at the beginning of June 1958. At first we were based at Tylosand, on the Swedish

Lurgan-born Billy Cush celebrates his 30th birthday in Sweden with Tommy Casey, Derek Dougan and me.

Riviera. It was about a four hours bus journey from Halmstad where our Group One matches were played. We stayed in a lovely hotel and, apart from our hard daily training sessions on a pitch surrounded by huge pine trees; we had a wonderful time. There was a lovely social club nearby and every time we entered the band struck up, 'When Irish Eyes are Smiling'. The Swedes were superb hosts. It was not always easy for us to leave that club early, but Peter Doherty and Gerry Morgan quietly saw to it that we did, not that we needed to be told, we were there to play against the best footballers in the world. We knew we had to discipline ourselves and maintain peak fitness to be able to compete with them. I think we showed the football world we could do just that, despite the frequent absence through injury of some of our key players. In the opening group we were up against Argentina, Czechoslovakia and West Germany.

On the eve of the first game against Czechoslovakia, Peter Doherty called the squad together at Halmstad. Tracksuited and puffing on his pipe he said, 'Remember you have a chance to achieve glory for yourselves, your country and for football.' He was a great motivator and on 8 June, Wilbur Cush scored the only goal in front of 20,000 in the Oerjansvall Stadium to get us off to the perfect start. We were the only British side to gain victory in the opening match. Doherty and Danny Blanchflower had watched the Czechs in Copenhagen and ensured they never got into their stride. Our long ball game constantly put them under pressure and Cush, who found the back of the net after fifteen minutes, formed a tremendous partnership on the right side with Billy Bingham. The man of the match was Bertie Peacock, as we had to defend pretty desperately in the second half, when a succession of free-kicks fully tested our defence. Of course, I was only a spectator at that game and the next two against Argentina and West Germany.

After that great win, our game against Argentina on 11 June was something of a disappointment. We started confidently enough and dominated the first half hour. After just four minutes, Peter McParland put us into a deserved lead with a header from Wilbur Cush's cross. However, the Argentineans closed down our wide players, forcing us to play through the middle, which proved much less effective. Their equalising goal came shortly before half-time from a penalty awarded for handling by Willie Cunningham, which knocked a lot of the fight out of us. Ultimately we were outplayed by very skilful ball players and two goals in six minutes early in the second half sealed their victory. Whilst Fay Coyle missed a sitter just before half-time, which could have changed things, were it not for Harry Gregg it could easily have been more. There was no shortage of effort and endeavour, although surprisingly Danny Blanchflower struggled again. Some people suggested it was because of what happened to his brother Jackie at Munich, but I think it was just a dip in form.

Of course, after the Argentina defeat the pressure was on us, as we had to get something out of our final Group game against the holders the following Sunday and we knew West Germany were no mugs. Even I couldn't relax, although I was a mere spectator. The then Governor of Northern Ireland, Lord Erskine, had flown in especially for the occasion. King Gustav of Sweden was also at our new venue, Malmo, and 8,000 of our fans from Halmstad made the one-hundred-mile journey to cheer us on. The team drew 2 – 2 and might well have won what is still remembered as one of the most breathtaking encounters of the tournament. It was undoubtedly Harry's match, despite being injured. He twisted his ankle in the opening minutes and hurt his shoulder, but time and time again he had the 22,000 crowd applauding his superlative saves, and half the crowd must have been German. His judgement and confidence had clearly fully returned following the trauma of Munich, and he was eventually rated the best goalkeeper of the tournament. Tommy Casey also suffered an early injury but, hobbling in midfield, it was from his pass to Billy Bingham that led to the opening goal after fifteen minutes. Billy's centre glanced Wilbur Cush's head and landed on Peter McParland's waiting foot. But within ninety seconds Uwe Seeler

Line up for the play-off against Czechoslovakia at Malmo in June 1958. Left to right: Danny Blanchflower, Willie Cunningham, myself, Wilbur Cush, Jimmy McIlroy, Billy Bingham, Jackie Scott, Bertie Peacock, Peter McParland, Dick Keith, Alf McMichael.

put Rahn in, and although Harry got his fingers to the ball, it went in off the post. Ten minutes into the second half a corner from Cush found Jimmy McIlroy, who touched it on to McParland, who made it 2 – 1. Just as it seemed we were heading for the quarter-final, a quick throw-in was pushed back to Seeler, who let fly from twenty-five yards, which gave Harry no chance.

The performance had put Northern Ireland football firmly on the map. We worked and tackled so hard and chased every ball – it was a wonderful team effort to the extent that Germany were happy for a draw and resorted to time-wasting tactics towards the end. Czechoslovakia secured an extraordinary 6 – 1 victory over Argentina, which meant we were up against them in a play-off to determine who would go through with the Germans to the quarter-finals.

Gerry Morgan had forty-eight hours to get Harry and Tommy Casey fit for the match against the Czechs again at Malmo on Tuesday 17 June. Tommy had four stitches in a gash on his right leg, together with a swollen ankle, and Gerry worked on both of them back at the hotel, but all to no avail. Jackie Scott came in for Tommy and I was back between the sticks for the most important game of my life.

The grass at Malmo was very thick and clingy and my injury jinx came back to haunt me after just ten minutes, when I twisted my left ankle very badly,

Gerry Morgan keeps my ankle working by pouring whiskey over it at frequent intervals – he used up two bottles!

which left me hobbling for the rest of the match. Shortly after, the Czechs, who had been the dominant team in the opening stages, scored. Feureisl and Willie Cunningham went up for a high ball, missed, and Zikan nipped in to nod past me. Gerry Morgan knelt down behind the goal during the first half and poured two bottles of Irish Whiskey around my ankle to try and keep the swelling down. As one of the newspapers wrote, 'What a waste of a good whiskey!' Peter McParland equalised on the stroke of half-time after three fierce shots from Wilbur Cash had been blocked and the ball finally fell loose to Peter.

The Czechs threw everybody forward at the start of the second half and I went in for a mad dive again, collided with Jan Dvorak and felt my left hand just go limp. It was broken, but somehow I was heading them out, catching them with one hand or putting them round the post. After ninety minutes the scores were level, so we went into extra time. After eight minutes, Danny Blanchflower curled a free-kick to the far post and Peter McParland calmly and majestically headed the winner for his fifth goal in three games. When Bubernik was sent off in fading light towards the end we knew the match was ours. It could have been different, as before the start of extra time I showed my swollen hand to Peter Doherty and suggested McParland go into goal. Peter said, 'Better not, Norman. I am confident you can hold them with just one arm and one leg.' I know I could never have scored a goal like our winner if I had gone outfield, so Peter's judgement and confidence was spot on again.

It was a hard, physical game, and in addition to my injury Bertie Peacock twisted a knee and had to go out on the left wing, with Wilbur Cush dropping back to left half. There was a disappointingly small crowd to witness one of our greatest wins, but there were wild scenes on the touchline from the Irish supporters at the end. Our team spirit was always in evidence, it was such a courageous effort, and overall, we played some excellent football and fully deserved to win. Despite my injuries I was very pleased with my own performance and rate it one of my finest. Indeed, 'Linesman' of Portsmouth headlined his report, 'Uprichard The Hero of Ireland's Great Win.'

The teams were:

Northern Ireland: Uprichard, Keith, McMichael, Blanchflower, Cunningham, Peacock, Bingham, Cush, Scott, McIlroy, McParland.
Czechoslovakia: Dolejsi, Mraz, Popluhar, Novak, Bubernik, Masopust, Dvorak, Molnar, Feureisl, Borovicka, Zikan.

For a while after the match, we locked the dressing room and savoured the greatest moment in Irish FA history. Peter Doherty lifted an empty lemonade bottle and cracked it against the massage table. The noise and singing momentarily stopped. His voice was loaded with emotion and words almost failed him. With tears in his eyes he managed to utter, 'Well done lads, you were magnificent.' We had a marvellous celebration prior to a four-hour bus ride back to our headquarters which we reached at 5 a.m. after some beer and many songs on the bus. I had my hand treated in hospital, but we had to leave for Norrkoping the next morning at 9.30 a.m.

Wales also pulled off a great result to reach the quarter finals by beating Hungary 2 – 1 in another play-off and were only eventually beaten by a Pele goal against Brazil. Our reward was a quarter-final against France two days after our epic victory. With my broken hand I knew my active part in the competition was over, but with just two keepers, Harry had to play more or less on one leg with a heavily strapped ankle. Bertie Peacock didn't make it and Tommy Casey wasn't fully fit. The game was played at Norrkoping and involved more travelling for us. Our team spirit kept us going for forty-five minutes, but we ran out of steam and France were worthy winners in the end by a 4 – 0 margin. Perhaps if we could have fielded our strongest side and all had been fit it might have been different. However, they had a fine team spearheaded by Juste Fontaine, who scored a hat-trick and Raymond Kopa knocked in the fourth. Both played magnificently and, after three glorious weeks in Sweden, our dream was over. But what an epic. When I think back it was unbelievable, a wee lad from Lurgan in County Armagh ending up playing at the World Cup.

In the dressing room after the match Peter Doherty made a speech praising us all and how far we had gone; not bad for a team labelled as the jokers in the pack. We asked the Irish Football Association if we could have the tracksuits we had worn in Sweden. The reply was 'sorry', we couldn't have them as they were needed for a youth international coming up soon. That was a very big disappointment. We thought the least they could have done was given us the tracksuits. I think there were quite a few hangers-on in those days as well. I still have my caps though. I was given a cap for each year that I played so received six caps in all. We had a lot of fun along the way and all gave 100 per cent for the green jersey.

Before we left for Stockholm airport the Swedish Football Association presented each of us with a beautiful cut glass memento with 'World Cup Sweden 1958' etched on it. The drama hadn't quite finished, as shortly after take-off we were calmly informed that the undercarriage of our plane was misbehaving. It had become stuck somewhere between being completely up and completely down. The captain, with what all of us later agreed was consummate professionalism and good humour, calmly announced, 'Eventually we will return to Stockholm but, before doing so, we will go on a sight-seeing trip up over the beautiful fjords of Norway. I want to use up most of the fuel and I'm not paying for it.' He may not have been paying, but most of us were praying. I can recall sweat dropping from dear Gerry Morgan's nose and a large succession of gin and tonics did much to help me come to terms with whatever destiny had laid out for us. In any event our pilot brought us down safely on a Stockholm airport runway flanked on each side by dozens of colourful fire engines and ambulances. We were shepherded from the plane to a VIP lounge in which BEA dispensed more and more refreshments, which of course we were happy to accept. Once we re-boarded a couple of hours later I promptly fell asleep and after what seemed like just a few minutes one of the air hostesses woke me up at Heathrow.

Most of us reached Ulster one way or the other. We had a wonderful welcome there, both collectively and individually. George Glass from Musgrave Park Hospital presented to us a set of statuettes of all our squad, which Danny Blanchflower accepted on our behalf.

To be fair to the IFA, they presented each of us with a gold watch shortly before the first home international match of the 1958–59 season against England. Nearer to home I also received a very nice letter from Mr W. G. Best, Town Clerk of Lurgan. My wage packet for the World Cup was £148 13s 9d. That represented four international fees as reserve at £30, £50 for playing against the Czechs plus two weeks wages from Portsmouth £34 less tax. It seemed like a fortune in those days!

Chapter Ten

Spanish Swansong

For myself and many others, the aftermath of our World Cup achievements didn't end there. Before we left Sweden we had received many invitations to play friendly matches against other countries, including Spain, and flew from London to Madrid in October 1958. I was selected as Harry Gregg, understandably, declined to go – the Munich disaster was still very fresh in his memory. The game took place at the famous Bernabeu Stadium of Real Madrid and it was nearly a disastrous trip for me, as three hours before the start I thought I would have to pull out. As we were in Spain I thought it only right to have a siesta in the afternoon and developed an excruciating pain in the small of my back, which had slightly twisted during the morning training session. When it woke me up I was practically paralysed. However, after some heat treatment from Gerry Morgan and a pain-killing injection, I was thankfully able to take the field. The crowd of 100,000 generated a terrific atmosphere – it was the largest gate I ever played in front of and seemed to inspire me. I would rate it as one of my top three performances, the other two being against Scotland at Windsor Park in 1955 and the Czechoslovakia play-off a few months before. The Spanish side contained a number of world class performers, seven of the all-conquering Real Madrid side, so it was no great surprise that we were beaten 6 – 2. I was kept very busy and the more I had to do, the more confident I became – it was one of those nights. I hated to be idle for periods in the game and often found in my career the more I was involved, the better my performance. At the end of the game the great di Stefano led me through a guard of honour formed spontaneously by the Spanish team – what a moment.

Sam Leith's report in particular gave me great pleasure – his headline was,

I marvelled tonight as 100,000 sporting Spaniards acclaimed Norman Uprichard, who surrendered six but stopped nearly sixty goals against the priceless supermen of Spanish football. The marvel was that the balding Alfredo di Stefano, supreme

The squad arrive at Madrid airport for the friendly against Spain. In the foreground myself (left), Gerry Morgan (centre) and Peter McParland (right).

I foil Luis Suarez in front of 100,000 spectators at the Bernabeu Stadium.

of an almost telepathic forward line, did not break the heart of this crew-cut 30 year-old Irishman. The mighty men of Spain ushered in Uprichard at the end and a standing roar from the appreciative Spaniards split the hot Madrid night – wonderful testimony to the Portsmouth man. This confident Spanish international team will surely trouble everyone they meet this season. They had Ireland stuttering helplessly within three minutes when a little black-haired bomb from Barcelona, right winger Mignel Tejada, shot the first of his four net-bulging goals. Even at full strength Ireland could not possibly have troubled the disciplined, daring Spanish. When you see precision football at twice the speed you see in England every Saturday, then you have some idea of the power and pace of Spain. Few defences in the world could master the cheeky, daring goal-grabbing power of Tejada, Kubala, di Stefano, Suarez and the world's fastest left winger Fransisco Gento.

Peter Doherty acknowledged,

Spain were a great team. On tonight's form no other country could have matched them.' For the record from a run by Billy Bingham Wilbur Cush scored after fifty minutes. Jimmy McIlroy, added a second twenty-six minutes later from Charlie Tully's corner. In his first international, Tommy Forde was facing di Stefano but acquitted himself well, tackling confidently and passing the ball sensibly. The Spaniards were on £250 bonus per man whereas of course we were again paid the usual international fee of £50.

Malcolm Brodie was very supportive of my efforts, headlining,

Uprichard is hero. Injustice if he's not chosen to play Scots. When Ireland's soccer selectors meet later this month to name their side to oppose Scotland, one name they must automatically put down is that of Norman Uprichard. In last night's 6 – 2 defeat by Spain under the floodlights of the Santiago Bernabeu Stadium, he was simply superb. "Magnifico, Magnifico, Magnifico!" cried the Spaniards as Uprichard gave them ninety minutes of spectacular goalkeeping of the calibre they like. Didn't he let in six goals? True but he must have saved dozens … no side could have lived with Spain last night … In conclusion last night was Norman Uprichard's night, the night he played himself back into our national side. He was the man who saved us from the hiding of a lifetime.

After publicly executing us on the field, the delightful, hospitable Spaniards laid on a seven-course banquet for us, during which we were each presented with a souvenir ash tray. It was a brilliant evening.

The teams were:

Northern Ireland: Uprichard, Keith, McMichael, Blanchflower, Forde, Casey, Bingham, Cush, McParland, McIlroy, Tully.

Spain: Alonso, Quinoces, Lesmes, Santisteban, Santamaria, Zarraga, Tejade, Kubala, di Stefano, Suarez, Gento.

Malcolm Brodie was spot on, as when the team to play Scotland at Hampden Park in November 1958 was announced I was back for my country. Typically, Harry Gregg was among the first to congratulate me. It lasted just one game, partly due to the brilliance of Harry, who was by then one of the finest keepers in the world, but also due to the extraordinary circumstances I faced when I returned to club football at Portsmouth. We started very slowly and were 2 – 0 down with goals from David Herd and Bobby Collins early in the second half before we really played with any great urgency. In fact it was only an own goal from full back Eric Caldow that enabled us to get back into the game. Billy Bingham hit an upright, Billy Simpson smacked the crossbar and a Bertie Peacock shot was cleared off the line before Jimmy McIlroy equalised with seven minutes to go. In the end a draw was a fair result and I was very happy with my performance.

Alan Dale headlined his report, 'Magnifico – that's just the word for Uprichard show'. An extract of Malcolm Brodie's report stated,

> The Irish defence mostly played with confidence and great positional sense. They were cool, calm and collected in most things they did. A mistake by Keith, who was slow to clear the ball, allowed Herd to get in a shot which carried immense power, but Uprichard saved magnificently ... For Norman it was a repeat of that magnificent form.

As a postscript to the wonderful time playing for my country, I must mention some of my fellow Irishmen who made my time with the Irish such an enjoyable experience. Firstly, trainer Gerry Morgan, one of the best men and greatest comedian's I have ever met in my life. He was always coming up with wisecracks like, 'Have you seen the new ten pound notes? I haven't seen the old ones yet!' or 'Have you cleaned the teeth today? Aye, both of them!' When you went down with a leg injury Gerry would rub the other leg and say, 'Come on son, get up, you are playing for your country.' Ireland owes an enormous debt to Gerry's boyish enthusiasm and sense of humour. The Irish squad only met three or four times every year but it was one of the finest squads in its history, in terms of spirit and camaraderie.

I make no apology for repeating my assertion that Peter Doherty was a complete footballing genius. Many who had the pleasure of playing with him, or witnessed him from the terraces, would argue that he was the greatest

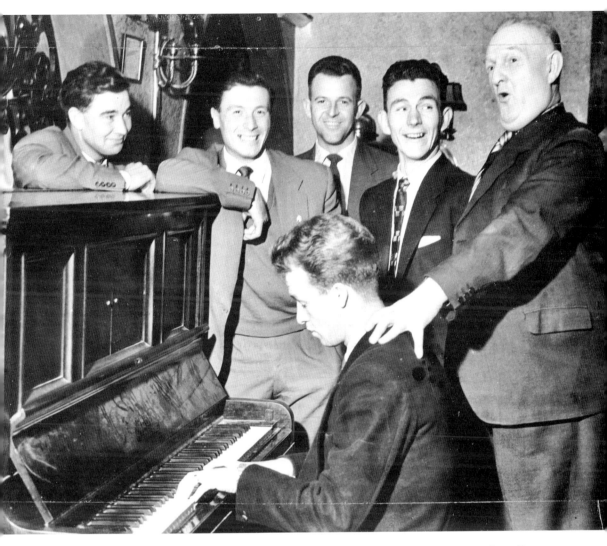

That wonderful character 'Uncle' Gerry Morgan (right), accompanied on the piano by Billy Bingham, supported by Jackie Blanchflower, Jimmy McIlroy, myself and Bertie Peacock.

inside-forward in the world at that time. He had all the necessary qualities of a thoroughbred – the acceleration of a greyhound, the body swerve of an eel, the ball control of a juggler, the shooting power of a Puskás, and the heading skill of a Tommy Lawton or Dixie Dean. He also had the uncanny ability of anticipation, being in the right place at the right time, and using superb dribbling skills, was able to release penetrating passes all over the park. In fact, apart from when he was playing for Derby with the great Raich Carter, his team mates were not always on the same wavelength, as he was ahead of his time.

In 1946, I watched an Ireland XI play a Combined Services XI at Windsor Park. Raich Carter was in the Combined Services team and Peter in the Ireland side. Frank Swift was in goal for the Services, who beat Ireland 8 – 4. Peter's performance that day was the greatest individual performance I have ever seen from a footballer. He scored all four goals for Ireland; one was a header from just outside the box. Frank Swift was no mug, a big goalkeeper, but Peter put it past him with ease. Raich Carter also scored four for the Services. I was standing close by when Peter came in at the end – saliva was all over his face; he had run himself into the ground. In many ways his skill and ball control reminded me of Alfredo di Stefano – and he wasn't too bad at cards either!

Alfie McMichael was my room-mate. He had big bushy ginger hair, but all of a sudden he started to go bald on the crown of his head. I used to say, 'Hey Alfie, there's a wee sixpence up there' and as time went on it became a shilling, then half a crown. I said I knew a hermit who lived in the hills in County Armagh who had a cure for baldness and would get him a bottle when I was next up there.

Finally Harry Gregg, a great friend, even bolder than me on the pitch, who has kindly written the foreword to this book, has provided these additional words:

We had three wonderful people at the time: Firstly, Peter 'The Great' Doherty, the greatest Irish footballer of all time, respected by his own players and the opposition of all nationalities. Peter was one of the first people to say football is a game of imagination and improvisation (as it is today), he was an unbelievable player, but also an inspirational leader and manager, ahead of his time. Bill Shankly used to call him the Ginger Tom, because he'd pop up with a pass here and there and then score a goal from nothing.

Peter took me from the backwaters of Ireland to Doncaster as a young man of nineteen. I shall never forget within a short while I was there seeing my first game under floodlights, a side of old internationals including Frank Swift, Raich Carter, Joe Mercer and Bill Shankly against a Doncaster team. For me, having read about them in the paper, it was an unbelievable spectacle watching these wonderful players. Then within two weeks Glasgow Celtic came down to play Doncaster as they wanted to see what it was like to play under lights and my name came up on the team sheet. Here I am playing against the great Celtic team I'd supported as a boy under lights, unbelievable.

Secondly, Danny Blanchflower, a marvellous talker, a very good player and our inspirational captain.

Thirdly, Gerry Morgan, who was at Nottingham Forest and won Irish international caps in his own time as a player, then became trainer at Linfield. Gerry carried a toothbrush in his top pocket and carried a comb, but he had neither hair nor teeth. That sounds ridiculous, but you're talking about a man who

Above: Training session at Largs in preparation for an away international against Scotland. From left: manager Peter Doherty, Billy Cush, Tommy Forde, Danny Blanchflower, Bertie Peacock, myself, Peter McParland, and trainer Gerry Morgan. In front are Willie Cunningham and Billy Simpson.

Right: Showing my injury prone right hand to a sympathetic young football supporter at Largs.

CLOSE UPS FOR HIS WIFE

IT was all because of his new television set. So cracked Norman Uprichard, Pompey's goalkeeper, after being knocked out three times while playing for Ireland against Scotland in yesterday's soccer international.

"I wanted my wife to see me on TV in close-ups," he said after the game.

Uprichard received a crack on the shoulder, a knock on the thigh, and a poke on the nose—but he'll be playing again on Saturday.

K.O. FOR 'KEEPER

Knocked out again in an international against Scotland.

would take all the drama out of a situation and all the pressure if such a thing existed in those days.

After each international match there was always a dinner where both teams would attend. The late, great, Sir Stanley Rous (I don't use the word great very often), a wonderful eloquent man, would always ask for Gerry to do a chat. Gerry would always say no, but Sir Stanley would persuade him and Gerry would 'do' the Grand National for him. He would pick up a glass tumbler and pretend it was a microphone.

Because I had been involved in an accident (Munich) in 1958 shortly before we went away for the World Cup, I travelled there by sea and land. A lot of people in Northern Ireland felt that we shouldn't be going to the World Cup, as some of the games might have to be played on a Sunday. But you have to be part of this crazy country to understand what that's all about. Because of the accident I went with a selector called Joe Beckett. When we eventually arrived in Sweden he immediately got on the plane and flew back to Ireland because of his religious beliefs in case he became 'contaminated'. Because of the accident I was told to room with Gerry – an unbelievable character. He would think nothing of throwing his coat down in the street in the middle of Stockholm and pretending he was a bookmaker, with all the lads having imaginary bets. And the public would look on thinking he was crazy.

Chapter Eleven

Black Jake and the Demon Drink

I have always taken a drink, sometimes one too many, but it has never ruled me. I could always take it or leave it. I know I had a bit of a reputation as a drinker, which is probably justified, but a lot of it was as a social drinker. I liked to celebrate success and enjoyed the company of people, as most Irishmen do. When we lost I drank to commiserate.

Mind you, it was at the tender age of fourteen, playing for St Peter's, that I had my first exposure to alcohol, something I grew rather partial to over the years, as my fellow pros would testify. We had a social club in a wee hut and used to invite Lurgan Harriers down to play darts. I met one of their members called Jim Crozier at the Castle Inn and he offered to buy me a pint. I said I didn't drink, but he bought me a pint of Porter, part of an Irishman's staple diet, now known of course as Guinness. Although I didn't like it, he got me another pint; I drank half and felt ill. I only lived about five minutes walk from the club and just about managed to get home drunk as a coot and rapped the front door. My mother took one look at me and hit me across the side of my face. I staggered upstairs and was sick all over the bed.

One might have thought it would put me off for life, but when I went to Distillery and we played at clubs like Coleraine, Ballymena and Crusaders, we usually had a pint after the games. I never drank Guinness again but stuck to beer.

At Arsenal, as at most clubs, training would finish at lunchtime. In the afternoons I didn't have much to do and Lily was at work. I got the tube down to the West End and had a look round, maybe having a pint or two. I knew the manager of the Manor House, Johnny Muir, who ran a dance upstairs. There was a big string orchestra that used to play and Lily and I often went there on a Saturday night for a few drinks.

At Swindon we always had a drink after the match at the County Hotel. George Hudson, Jimmy Paine, Maurice Owen and me were the regulars. There were few Irish people living at Swindon at the time, but we had some good nights and it never affected my play. One of the directors, Freddie Fox, had a pub about 100 yards from the ground and during the week after a few games of snooker in the social club, I'd call in for a couple of pints. I played a lot of darts at Swindon, every Sunday morning at the Carpenters Arms in Gorse Hill, near where I lived, with a few pints to steady my hand.

I never heard anyone make a rule about not drinking before a game, but I never drank on a Thursday or Friday night. I should qualify my comments, as there was just one exception at Portsmouth when I did go on the field with drink inside me from the night before. Offenbach Kickers, a German team, played a friendly match against us. I received a letter from a bloke from Lurgan to say he was in the Army and was being moved to the RAOC at Hilsea Barracks, just on the outskirts of Portsmouth. There was a big social night at his barracks which he invited me to, so the night before the game Duggie Reid, Johnny Gordon and me went to the Sergeant's Mess, where we were given coupons for drinks. I had more drinks than planned and in the morning didn't feel too bright. I went for a walk along the seafront to try and clear my head, then had a cup of tea and a bit of toast as usual. When I reached the ground at about 1.45 p.m. Phil Gunter said I smelt like a brewery. I said I felt like one! We beat them 1 – 0, the Doog scored the goal, but Eddie Lever said it was such a disgraceful performance everyone had to report for extra training on Monday, except me, who played a blinder! Is there a moral there? I'm not sure.

After my second game for Portsmouth, when my hand was smashed at Sheffield Wednesday, I travelled back via Paddington and arrived at about midnight into Swindon. Dougie Woolcroft, who was a wheel tappers mate at Great Western Railways, had invited me to a big party for the station staff. I thought a few drinks would help dull the pain and got home at about 2.30 a.m. Somehow, I had to get to Portsmouth the next day for them to look at my injury. Dougie's brother, Cliff, who was a bookmaker, lived two doors away and agreed to drive me to Portsmouth. Eddie Lever got it X-rayed and I found out all the breaks and had it put into plaster. It was quite a weekend. Cliff drove me to various village pubs on Sunday mornings, like Marlborough, where he'd settle up his accounts and we'd always end up half pissed.

Portsmouth was a bigger town, a bigger world than the one I was used to, and the tension and pressure of playing First Division football got to me. I dreaded the build up to a game and particularly Friday night, as I played the match over two or three times in my mind. What if I made a mistake in front of 30,000 people? What would they think? I was a bad sleeper, but I wasn't physically sick and once on the pitch, and the whistle went, I was fine. After the anxiety of a match I'd have a few drinks to relax, drown my sorrows or celebrate. When we played Arsenal I was always more nervous than any other teammate, because it was where I started in England. On the morning of the home match against the Gunners in March 1958, I went for a good walk along the seafront to the Devonshire Arms, where I saw a couple of mates playing cards. I ordered a glass of orange squash and played cards with them to help ease my nerves, then walked to Fratton Park. It was a wonderful game, we beat them 5 – 4 with goals from Johnny Gordon (2), Peter Harris, Mike Barnard and Derek Dougan. I was on a high until someone said they had seen me drunk in the Devonshire Arms before the game and because of my reputation reported me to Eddie Lever. I explained to Mr Lever how nervous I was and he accepted my explanation, but I wonder if there were any lingering doubts. Certainly rumours about me drinking before a match were completely unfounded.

There have been various explanations about my nickname of 'Black Jake'. Monday was usually our day off at Portsmouth, and I used to play snooker regularly. I'd been on a bit of a binge this particular weekend, had been drinking the night before and was still half pissed I think. I hadn't had a shave and went to the snooker hall with a beard. In those days my hair was black so I looked like a bit of a scruffy pirate. I played against Jimmy Scoular for a few bob and won most of the games. The last game we put more money in and everything I potted went in. Jimmy called me 'Black Jake' after the pirate in *Swallows and Amazons*, who took all the money. It stuck with my teammates ever since.

In the foreword Harry Gregg thought my nickname originated from my lift in a coal lorry. I think he was referring to the time Pompey had a game at Preston on a Saturday and I was playing against Scotland at Hampden Park the following Wednesday. It was my responsibility to get transport from Preston to Glasgow. I had a bit of time to spend at Preston, so walked into a pub and somebody called out 'Hiya Norm'. It was a bloke called Jackie Long, known as Shorty, who I knew from Lurgan. He was working there and we had a few drinks and something to eat before I realised it was midnight. So, I had to catch the last train, which was a coal train. I was put into a little carriage, which was pretty dirty and uncomfortable. I arrived covered in black and the boys took the piss out of me. Jimmy McIlroy has a variation on the story and I understand even Alex Elder, another wonderful Irish footballer, but someone who broke into the international side after I had retired, has been told my nickname dates back to a lift on a coal lorry to an international, but it is not so.

There were many temptations to partake in the demon drink at Portsmouth. I got to know one of the managers of a local brewery, who used to invite me down to one of his pubs. After training I'd go to his office and he'd get out a crate of beer and a couple of glasses and we'd have a few beers for a couple of hours. I'd go home for dinner then be back out to the pub for another couple of jars and a few games of darts. I played so much that I managed quite a few 180s in my time. I was at the Devonshire Arms one evening in 1958, as normal, for a pint and a game of cards with the locals when Johnny Gordon came in, which was a surprise as he never used the pub but knew I did. 'I've just been transferred to Birmingham,' Johnny said. He mentioned he'd got a few bob out of the transfer so I challenged him to 301 at darts for a treble rum. I threw double 11, 1 and triple top 60. Then I scored a ton to leave me wanting 118. Treble 16, treble 10 and double top, thanks Johnny!

On Mondays, Tuesdays and Wednesdays we also got into the habit of going out for a few drinks at the Alma Arms, playing cards until closing time then walking home. My drinking companions were usually Johnny Gordon, Jackie Henderson, Gordon Dale and Derek Rees. It was all innocent fun and helped us bond into such a good team.

Chapter Twelve

Slippery Descent into Non-League Football

Following the traumatic events at Portsmouth when Freddie Cox released me, it proved difficult to find another league club. Maybe I had a reputation as a trouble-maker after speaking out in the newspapers, maybe I had a reputation as being difficult, argumentative or even an Irish boozer, I will never know. Perhaps it was felt that I was past my prime. Nowadays of course, goalkeepers play in the league well into their thirties and some peak through experience late in their career. It was, however, different in the 1950s and I needed a new club to survive financially. I had little to fall back on and the maximum wage had yet to be abolished.

In truth, age and countless injuries were fast catching up with me. Watford were initially interested and a part-exchange deal with centre-forward Bobby Howfield was being lined up, but fell through. Then Third Division Southend United came in for me, which I was pleased about as I was used to living by the sea and they offered me top wages. I was transferred for £1,500 on 6 July 1959, but at thirty-one I knew I had begun my descent down football's ladder.

I was in the first team for about twelve games when once more my title as the unluckiest goalkeeper in the game was further enhanced. We were winning 1 – 0 at Reading when in the second-half a corner came in from the left. They had a centre forward called Bill Lacey, a big, strong, hard, typical lower league player. I went up for the ball and he hit me with everything he had. He didn't miss me and I ended up in the back of the net with my left arm broken. I wasn't a big keeper but could hold my own. However, he hit me when I was off the floor and my arm was hanging limp. I had a compound fracture and was out until after Christmas.

It was so painful initially that I slept on the armchair, as I couldn't lie on it in bed. Just as I was about to come back, I poured a cup of tea all over my arm, which blistered and put me out for another three weeks. Our manager, Eddie Perry, was a decent man and I felt sorry for him that I couldn't return until Easter

1960, when we were struggling to avoid relegation. We won the four matches over Easter but poor Eddie, knowing how accident prone I was put me on the transfer list. I didn't blame him.

Whilst no other league clubs were interested, Hereford and Hastings came in for me. Tim Kelly, the manager of Southern League Hastings, met me in the 1960 close season at Charing Cross station over a cup of coffee. We talked terms and I signed as a part-timer for £17, which was only £3 less than my wages in the First Division, £15 in the summer and £2 bonus plus a job, which all together was more money than if I played full time. I played with Len Duquemin, the old Spurs forward in the first season and had a good laugh with him; he was another comedian.

Once again my bad luck soon struck. After just three games for Hastings, we played at Guildford in October and near the end of the match as usual I went in head first and came out feeling my right knee wasn't right. I went for an X-ray the following morning and they diagnosed cartilage, so I had my cartilage taken out and made slow progress. I was out for several weeks, running up and down the terracing until I started to play again. Sussex county cricketer Graham Cooper proved a worthy deputy in goal, but by the time I returned we were bottom of the Premier Division. At the end of the season I got a letter from the club stating, 'Owing to the finances of the club, we no longer require your services. Please vacate your flat by June 30th.' The rent for the clubhouse on the sea front was seven guineas a week, I was on £12–13 a week as a labourer, so it was going to leave about £35 a week to feed and clothe three small kids. I was never one for saving but had £1,100, which would keep us going for a while. But I thought I'd spent enough time in bars on the outside to know a bit about pubs, so I thought I'd try and get a tenancy. So I made a few enquiries and applied to a brewery broker, got a letter back, had an interview and we secured the Belmont Pub at Hastings in June 1961. It was a run-down pub but I built it up and enjoyed it almost as much as being between the sticks. We introduced bar billiards and darts, and it became a sports and social place rather than just a pub. My mother also came to live with us there for over ten years. I was happy in my new career and many old friends from all over the place dropped in for a chat and a pint.

Then Ramsgate, another Southern League club, persuaded me to play for them in August 1961 for £27 per week plus expenses. I had a year at the pub and playing at Ramsgate, but found it very difficult to do both. I trained by running up and down the beach and actually managed a season injury free. The last press report I have was against Trowbridge in early 1962:

Uprichard was brilliant – Irish wizard saves a point. Ramsgate, like Trowbridge, are still in the Southern League Division One promotion hunt and the tough, unceremonious battle which ensued at Frome Road on Saturday was not surprising. The Rams did well to get away with a valuable point although they never looked in serious difficulties until the last fifteen minutes. Then Norman Uprichard, who had almost been a spectator, had one of the busiest spells of his non-league career. It was only his amazing anticipation and swiftness which kept Trowbridge from snatching a late victory ... Spectators saw Uprichard show some of his old international form. In rapid succession he kept out close range shots from Akers and Coggins. Seconds later Pullman met a centre first-time only to find that Uprichard had anticipated the direction and scooped the ball round the post. Almost on time, Baker got in a low shot well on target but again the marvellous Uprichard brought the house down by diving on the ball to save.

The 'house' consisted of 950 spectators.

At the end of the 1961–62 season I knew my serious football career really was over. The Belmont was taking up more and more of my time. I did find time to run a junior league in Hastings and even played a few games for Hastings Rangers. Even then I managed to knock my collar bone out against Newhaven, so went on the wing and scored a goal. I had no regrets, it was fun while it lasted, despite all the injuries and I'm glad I played during the period I did. My sporting interests gradually transferred to angling, golf, darts, billiards and snooker. I once won the Hastings individual darts cup and was a member of the team that won the Hastings and District snooker league and knock-out cup.

In October 1962, I went to White Hart Lane to watch my beloved Glasgow Rangers play Spurs in the European Cup Winners' Cup. I bumped into Alex Govan, who played for Plymouth when I broke my ribs in 1951. When I mentioned I was now a publican he said so was he, in Plymouth. I gave him my business card, which was a Guinness beer mat! Alex played with me for a short time at Portsmouth; he was a very good outside left and scored a lot of goals for a winger, including a hat-trick against me for Plymouth reserves when he was coming back from injury.

I left Hastings after running the pub for seven years in 1968 as Lily wanted to go back to Ireland. Her parents were getting on a bit and her sister Sadie wanted her to return too, so I got out of the pub and we found a house in the Ormeau Road in Belfast. We were only back a couple of weeks and I got a job in a pub called Temple House in East Belfast as charge hand in an area where they were all Glentoran supporters. But right in the middle, there were a few Linfield supporters. All the Linfield supporters used Temple House, known as the Blue Bar, as Linfield played in blue. Lily got a job in town at a very busy bar called King Richard Tavern via an old friend of mine Clancy McDermott, who played for Fulham and Glentoran. She had previous experience behind the bar in Hastings.

'Mine Host' with Lily at the Belmont Arms in Hastings in 1966, World Cup year.

'Professor' Cullen, a popular fortune teller on Hastings pier during the holiday season, admires my collection.

A return between the sticks at Fratton Park in 1974.

Then, I was appointed manager of the Raven Bar in Ravenhill Road. My ambition was to make the Raven the 'Rangers' bar of East Belfast and I think I achieved something in that direction. I also became Glasgow Rangers scout in Ulster but, by the very nature of my job, my scouting activities were restricted and I regrettably had to resign. I always had three ambitions in life – to play for Ireland, Arsenal and Rangers. Jerry Dawson, the Glasgow Rangers goalkeeper when I was a child, was always my idol and I wanted to follow in his footsteps, but never quite made it.

I was doing a few turns for a pub at the top of the Shankhill Road in Belfast called The Top House when one evening on the way to work a bullet flew over my shoulder about two feet above my head. I dived into a shop and stayed there for about twenty minutes until the shooting stopped. On another occasion I was on the bus and two masked armed men leapt out and stopped it. The driver and passengers were ordered out; the tyres were shot to pieces and the bus used as a barricade. At once Saracen armoured cars were on the scene and all hell broke loose. We lay on the pavement and hoped for the best. Even allowing for the

A reunion at Dunmore Stadium, Belfast, for the 1979 National Sprint Final with some of the greats of Irish football. From left: Joe Bambrick, myself, Jimmy Jones, Bertie Peacock, Jimmy McAlinden and Tommy Breen.

sectarian violence in Belfast in the 1970s, I never regretted my decision to return to Ireland. I was brought up as a Protestant, but had as many Catholic friends in Lurgan as Protestant. It has never bothered me what religion a person is, as long as they didn't try to influence me, I have always been able to form an opinion without anyone else's help. So I never had any trouble personally, but sometimes you can be in the wrong place at the wrong time.

After the Top House I worked at Belfast Corporation Transport Club for a few years, a club for bus drivers, etc. Finally, I had a job as a steward at Queen's University in the Common Room, serving all the professors, etc. I stayed there for twelve and a half years and enjoyed it; it gave me plenty of opportunity for having a few drinks. It was within walking distance from our house or I would catch the bus and stagger home. Then our eldest daughter Pauline was expecting a baby back in Hastings and wanted her mum over and, as I had probably got into a bit of a rut, she went ahead of me while I sold the house and cleared up, and followed her back to Hastings. The University had a big afternoon for me

Working behind the bar in Queen's University Common Room, Belfast, in 1980.

when I left and presented me with £2,000, which in 1984 was a tidy sum. They must have thought a lot of me.

When I was at Queen's University I received a letter out of the blue from my old Portsmouth teammate Jack Mansell, who was managing the Israel national side at the time. Israel were playing Northern Ireland in a World Cup tie at Belfast and Jack wanted me to be with the party and help with the pre-match organisation. No way was I going to help them beat my country so, whilst I helped smooth the way for Jack and his team, football advice was out of the question.

Back in England, in 1984, I got a bar steward job at the old Hastings Club in the High Street, but the secretary at the time was not a nice man. I stuck it until I slipped over an orange peel in the store and did my back in. My doctor said not to hump any more cases and signed me off indefinitely in 1992. Since then my health has not been brilliant and I have been relying on benefits.

All the while I was trying to keep involved in football. When Peter Doherty was at Preston North End I introduced one or two Irish lads to him, but they didn't quite make it. I did a bit of scouting for Brian Clough at Derby County

Lily and me enjoying retirement.

while I was in Belfast, but couldn't get them any decent players. Then I wrote to Glasgow Rangers offering to scout and did that for a season. It got me out and about watching games and they signed a couple of lads but they weren't good enough. I have a letter from Peter when he was at Preston in 1972. He says, 'I termed you as my most courageous goalkeeper,' which makes me feel very humble coming from such a great man.

I get regular invites back to Portsmouth, they always keep in touch, which is tremendous, and occasionally to Arsenal, but have only been back to Swindon once when they played Portsmouth in the cup. I have been back to Ireland quite a few times at the invitation of the Irish FA, the latest in 2008 when six of us survivors were presented with a plaque at the Sports Writers' Association annual dinner in Belfast to mark the 50th anniversary of the 1958 World Cup Finals. We were given a standing ovation by the crowd at half-time in the Ireland game against Czech Republic, which was very gratifying after all these years. The survivors from 1958 still keep in touch with each other, and that's what I call real camaraderie.

With granddaughter Francoise.

With granddaughter Maria, who sadly passed away in 2005 at the age of twenty-eight.

Above: Stephen with his two sons, Stuart and Stephen.

Right: A present from the Irish FA presented in 2008 on the 50th anniversary of the World Cup Finals.

Above: A family photograph with our two daughters and son taken in about 2001.

Left: Pauline's son Stephen.

Grandchildren Darren, Lucy and Lee.

My two daughters, Jill and Pauline.

The St Peter's Gaelic medal I finally received in 2004.

Proudly sporting my Northern Ireland goalkeeping kit.

One of my closest friends in the game was Derek Dougan, 'The Doog', who arrived at Portsmouth from Distillery. He was flamboyant, with a big sports car, and if you didn't know him you would say he was big-headed and arrogant, but that wasn't right, as he would do anything for anybody and was a very nice fella. I knew his father very well too, as I worked with him as a labourer for a short time when I went back to Belfast at Harland & Wolff. When the Doog came to the club from East Belfast, he was packed on a boat and had no idea where Portsmouth was, never having had a geography lesson in his life. So I took him under my wing, being ten years older. We used to go for a cup of tea and chat after training, and I saw him blossom over the years.

In early 2007, Derek came down with his partner Merlyn, a very nice girl, to help me at an industrial tribunal in Eastbourne because of my football injuries, but as there was some missing documentation it had to be postponed. Then the day before he was due to return in June 2007 I had a phone call from Merlyn to say the Doog had a heart attack. It was such a shock as I had only spoken to him a couple of days previously. Then at the tribunal I wasn't able to put forward my argument very effectively with the shock of Derek's death, so contrary to some press reports, the case wasn't concluded satisfactorily and a lump sum I had hoped for never materialised.

My family means the world to me and has always been supportive, particularly since Lily's death. We had three children, Stephen, who lives in Bury, and Pauline and Jill, who both live locally. Stephen's partner is Diana. He has two sons, Stephen and Stuart, and two daughters, Francoise and Maria, who sadly passed away. Pauline is married to Tracy and has two children, Stephen and Lucy. Jill is married to Jim and has two boys, Lee and Darren.

All my grandchildren drive but I never had the inclination to drive. Wherever I played, I lived a short distance from the ground. I've never had a car nor taken a lesson, but walked everywhere – I was always too fond of having a drink!

I've had a difficult time with my health over the last year in particular. Towards the end of 2010, I had a toe amputated, which took a while to get over. Then in December 2010 my beloved Lily passed away and I couldn't go to the funeral as I was back in hospital with concerns about the circulation in my leg. The day after the funeral I had a bypass in my leg and I've had marvellous support from the family. I have always been blessed with a good memory and have enjoyed reliving my life and career with the help of Chris. It has brought back so many memories and made me realise how lucky I have been. I played over 260 games in English senior football and experienced the joy of walking out at Windsor Park packed with 51,000 fans and Hampden with its 100,000 – unforgettable. I've made some wonderful friends both in England and back in my native Ireland, and I wouldn't change anything if I had my time again.

Epilogue

Norman enjoyed reminiscing about his footballing days and life in general. He had a wonderful memory, and was very much looking forward to the publication of this book. Sadly he passed away at a Brighton hospital on 31 January 2011, so it was not to be. I hope the book provides a flavour of social context for players of Norman's era, where they played football not for the money, but because they loved the sport and were extremely good at it. It was a privilege and pleasure to work with him on this book and I hope Norman's words prove a worthy legacy to a fascinating life.

Looking through Norman's papers I discovered the following poem about the 1958 World Cup Finals. It was written by Arthur Clarke in 1980 and encapsulates Norman as a person and a top-class goalkeeper.

Norman the Brave

How can we forget his exploits
For it doesn't seem that long ago
That a goalkeeper named Norman Uprichard
Was to set our hearts aglow.

With damaged hands and aching limbs
And his body black and blue
His only thought was that day
To see Northern Ireland through.

For he was a man who stood alone
Out there on a patch of green
Reminding me once again
Of the greatest I have seen.

To me this holds a great memory
That I have stored away
For this was a piece of treasure
To remember every day.

So always look back to 1958
For you will surely find
That from your boyhood dreams
The world became all thine.

Well Norman always keep this memory
For the football world knows your name
But I know one thing for certain
You're first in my hall of fame.

Norman was a courageous performer and a courageous man to the end. His funeral took place on Monday 14 February 2011 at Hastings Crematorium, where his son, Stephen, delivered a moving eulogy, and Portsmouth Football Club historian Richard Owen covered Norman's career. On behalf of the Irish Football Association the funeral was attended by Roy Cathcart, who handed Norman's daughter, Jill, a tankard that was scheduled to be presented to Norman towards the end of 2010 at the Italy international.

Norman's intention was to dedicate the book to Lily, his wife of sixty-two years, who was struck down by Alzheimer's, that cruellest of illnesses. I would like to dedicate it to both Norman and Lily, with thanks to their full and varied lives.

Chris Westcott

Tributes to Norman from the Family and Football Fraternity

Stephen (son)

I am a socialist and one of the very first injustices I felt in life relates to my father. I went to school as usual in January 1958, the day of the vital World Cup qualifier against Italy. Manchester was fog-bound and Harry Gregg couldn't get over to play, so my father played. A teacher from another class came into our room and said in front of thirty other children, 'Stephen's father is playing in the international.' I knew it was such an important match as it was being shown live on television, and was very excited, but they didn't even let me off for the afternoon. I would have loved to have seen my father help the team win but nobody said, 'Stephen you can go home and watch the match.' Even as a seven-year-old boy I felt that wasn't quite right. My schooling that afternoon wasn't as important as the match, and it made a deep impression of the injustice on me.

Unfortunately I didn't have the natural talent, or good eyes of my father, but I have always enjoyed sport, particularly cricket, but only up to a certain standard. I saw my father play many times at Fratton Park. Even though Portsmouth were in the First Division I remember there was only one player, Jimmy Dickinson, at the club with a car, the rest would go to the match on public transport. Dad was very popular with the crowd at Fratton Park and they used to throw him chocolate bars into the net before the start. I remember on a Saturday night, whether or not I'd been to the game, he would bring the bars home, which is not something you would see nowadays.

Pauline (daughter)

I have no idea why dad was called Norman, as opposed to William; I think he just preferred it, he was always known as Norman. He was just the way he was, he didn't take after anybody. He had a typical Irish jovial sense of humour with a twinkle in his eye. He used to walk us to the seafront for ice-creams every week from the Belmont pub where we lived. We walked down Harold Road to the café on the seafront which Tilly Di Marco, his friend, owned. He would leave us eating Knickerbocker Glory's while he went to pay his bills and I think, secretly also went to the bookies. Dad knew Tilly as a fellow businessman in the town and being an Italian, he was naturally interested in football. My first memories were living in the flat above the pub; dad had hung his boots up by then. He used to open at midday lunchtime, and then close the doors at two – except for his regular, select, Irish and Scottish local community, when he would have a lock-in – they didn't always happen in Ireland! I hated living there because it wasn't like a normal house. For example, you could only get to the garden through the cellar – it just wasn't normal. I used to say to Mum, 'Can't we have a house like everybody else?' One day I packed my suitcase and went round to my friend Jenny's. I was leaving home, I was only about eight but I did come back!

Jill (daughter)

Dad was always there to help us, financially, or if any of us were in any trouble. He was loving and generous, especially to his grandchildren, and looked after them when we worked. He'd take them to school then collect them later in the day and often went out with them on a Sunday to the park to feed the ducks. As they got older and became interested in snooker and pool mum and dad would take them down to the angling club. He always said they were his happiest days. They were very good grandparents, and as mum and dad they were great parents.

SWINDON TOWN

Sam Burton

Norman was an international who knocked me out of the Swindon team until he was transferred to Portsmouth. When I saw one of the floodlight pylons in the corner at Swindon on the television recently it reminded me when I climbed up it one day when they first put them up and the manager appeared. Of course the boys wouldn't tell him where I was and I had to stay up the top for what seemed a long time until he had gone. We had some fun with Norman, who lived the other side of Swindon, so I didn't see much of him away from the County Ground. I seem to recall he used to go out drinking with our winger Jimmy Bain, who eventually went to Australia.

George Hudson

Norman was an outstanding goalkeeper and particularly good coming off his line at corners. Being a centre-half I appreciated that. He was very confident, which in turn gave us confidence. He was quite a character, along with Sam Burton and Maurice Owen, which gave us a great team spirit at the time.

PORTSMOUTH FC

Bill Albury

During the two seasons I played in the first team, Jimmy Dickinson and Jimmy Scoular were the mainstays. About the only time youngsters like me had a chance of playing was if someone broke a leg. I certainly didn't get a chance, even if the first team lost. I could play full back or wing half and because of my versatility often travelled with the team, but only played if someone was sick overnight. I remember the Manchester United victory (October 1957) like it was yesterday; playing at Old Trafford was the highlight of my career. I marked Dennis Viollet; we were 3 – 0 up at half-time and didn't want the game to stop. We knew they'd come at us in the second half but we stood firm – Norman played brilliantly. Back in Portsmouth after the coach journey I was walking home at about 2 a.m. when I was stopped by a copper, who shone a torch in my face and said stroppily, 'What have you got in that bag?' I was tired and all I wanted to do was get into bed. When I told him I'd been playing for Pompey at Manchester United and showed him my blazer underneath my jacket, of course he changed his tune. He didn't worry about my bag – all he wanted to do was talk about football. My bonus for that win was £4!

I shared a room with Norman once overnight, which we rarely did on away games as it was usually straight on the coach and back to Portsmouth. Norman was an excellent shot stopper, but because of his height – or lack of it – rarely came off his line. He was the same height as me at 5 feet 9 inches. He wasn't big enough to always come out and punch it from corners or free kicks. Like Norman I also had a ruck with Freddie Cox – everyone fell out with him. Eight of us all left Pompey together, I was not impressed and off I went to Gillingham.

There were so many aspects of the game that were different in those days. My wages were £14 a week in the winter, £12 in the summer with a part-time job to pay our way. Our diet was also different, for me it was usually poached egg on toast or a bit of fish, as my tummy started to churn before a game. We went to the match on a Corporation bus with the spectators; it was unbelievable when you think about it now. I sat playing cards four days out of five with Jimmy Dickinson in a café round the corner after training. Most of us didn't have cars; Mike Barnard had one as did Jimmy Dickinson, who lived at Alton. Jimmy had to get permission to drive backwards and forwards every day for training. You weren't allowed to own or drive a motor bike and there was no dancing after Mondays. We had to be indoors by 10.30 a.m. every night during the week. Cliff Parker, the old outside left who scored for Pompey in the 1939 FA Cup final, was one of our trainers – he used to take the 'A' team and reserves. He came round and knocked on the door to make sure I was in by 10.30 a.m.

Norman was a wonderful man, and we used to have a laugh. It wasn't the money, it was the comradeship.

Mike Barnard

Norman was a first-class goalkeeper playing in what is now the Premiership. When he was injured against Nottingham Forest for the reserves I went in goal because my specialist position for Hampshire at cricket was at first slip and they thought I'd be a reasonable deputy when Norman was injured. I used to live in Havant and went to a firm just outside town that produced this special sheepskin glove for Norman to play in, which he found comfortable and warm. Under Freddie Cox my job in the First Division was to stay wide on the half-way line, get hold of any loose balls and kick it into the penalty area – high-class technical stuff. I think he got his job on the back of Bournemouth beating Tottenham in the Cup.

Jack Mansell

Norman was someone who probably gave neither goalkeeping nor anything else much thought. He was just a happy go lucky person, not serious about much, and the number one character at the club. He was very lively in the dressing room and very lively outside it too. I think he spent quite a few Saturday evenings fairly horizontal. He was a natural, very brave, and had the basic gifts of a goalkeeper, as he had a good pair of hands, was courageous, had a good knowledge of angles, was good with crosses and a good shot stopper. As he wasn't a big man, he relied entirely on timing and deciding when to come off his line. His favourite word was 'Shoot' as when forwards had the ball in an advantageous position Norman would shout 'Shoot!' and they would shoot from a distance, he almost told them when to hit the ball. On a match day he'd come to the ground about as late as you could, got changed in about three minutes, played the match, had a shower and went home. He didn't live and breathe football and didn't think greatly about the game. I was always interested in coaching, but I couldn't see that in Norman. He was 'salt of the earth' and I liked him.

Tommy McGhee

Norman was a character, a very good dart player, and he liked a drink – which we all did. At times he took it to excess and was a bit of a wild boy off the pitch. He also liked a gamble on fixed odds football coupons. In Portsmouth the supporters in the city were so fanatical, if Norman went into a pub for a quiet drink and nobody recognised him, he'd tell them who he was instead of keeping his mouth shut! My full-back partner Jack Mansell was another character. He kept himself to himself, but even then he was interested in coaching and was only thirty-one when he went to Eastbourne United as player-manager.

Norman was a very good keeper for his size; he was not much taller than me at 5 feet 8 inches, compared with Frank Swift, for example, who was a giant. I remember watching Frank, who was a PT instructor at my school, play for Manchester City against Arsenal. There was a big fella called Doug Lishman who was injured and Frank picked him up and carried him off the pitch like a baby. Because of his lack of height Norman could get a bit timid as the goalies weren't protected as they are today. If he went up for a ball big forwards like Nat Lofthouse or Trevor Ford would knock him, but he'd still turn in a performance. He tried to bribe Trevor Ford once with tickets for his friends before he played against Sunderland. We told Norman they wouldn't take any notice of him. He got up well and wasn't frightened of coming out as far as the penalty spot. When Norman was out of the side we struggled. I remember in 1957 we lost 4 – 1 to Nottingham Forest. Eddie Baily was playing for them and said, from his experience, at Tottenham a good goalie is worth two goals. Norman was as safe a goalkeeper as you could find in those days.

We had a director whose mother owned Chapman's laundry down Kingston Crescent. Your money as a pro went down in the summer so I asked the director if there was any work about. He had a few words and Norman and I took a job there. They did the washing for all the holiday camps on Hayling Island, etc. It wasn't like today, all the sheets from the bedding were put into huge washing machines – they didn't spin the washing like nowadays. Norman worked hard, I was fortunate. I weighed in the dry washing in big barrels with someone else and just pushed the trolley, etc., it was easy. Poor Norman was put on a massive spin drier and would have to pull the wet washing out of the machine, and with his injured hands Norman really grafted. It made you appreciate how fortunate you were being a footballer. It was a forty-eight-hour week and if there wasn't enough work come Friday they'd let you go. You clocked off and wouldn't get paid for any hours not worked. We were paid about £7 per week in the laundry which went towards the rent on our house. We used to cycle to the laundrette and I was behind Norman once when somebody opened a car door and knocked him off his bike. He was fortunate as he could have broken his wrist, but he dusted himself down and got back on his bike. We only did it for one summer, and that was enough!

We all fell out with Freddie Cox – he was the man who ruined Portsmouth Football Club. When I was in the Combination side I was selected for a representative XI to play in Holland which Eddie Lever managed. Another Irish goalkeeper from Bournemouth called Tommy Godwin played. We knew Cox was coming to us at the time and Tommy was so thankful Cox was leaving Bournemouth. He said he was a terrible man and had a lot of sympathy for us. He told us, 'I go to training on a bike and by the time I've finished I have to push it home I haven't got the energy to cycle, he worked us so hard.' Then Cox came here and brought with him a terrible Scottish trainer called Dougie Davidson, and he was the most foul-mouthed man I've ever heard in my life. When we played at Blackpool I was the 12th man sat in the dug-out, and the spectators were standing on the terraces almost on top of us. When Davidson started swearing I said, 'Here Doug, there's ladies there.' He said they shouldn't be there.

Before Cox came, when we played away we travelled by first-class rail and stayed in first-class hotels. He put a stop to that and we travelled third class until one of the directors pointed out in the minutes that all the while Portsmouth were in the First Division the first team would travel first class. If you were playing away he would always take us to the pictures even if we'd arrive at eight and the film started at seven. If a couple of us got fed up and walked out we made sure we went in different directions, so he couldn't follow both of us!

Prior to playing Burnley in the fifth round of the FA Cup in February 1959, we were taken to Butlins at Saltdean near Brighton for training. Phil Gunter told me that in the local paper it stated that ginger (me) was being replaced by ginger (Alex Wilson) – we both had ginger hair. I confronted Cox and when I asked if I was in the team he said he hadn't made up his mind yet. I knew he had but he didn't have the guts to tell me. I told him I wasn't travelling to Burnley as the

12th man, but would play in the reserves instead. He said it was only a friendly match, but that was good enough for me. We lost the game 1 – 0 and I only played once more for him, a 4 – 4 draw at Spurs.

Cox bought players from the Third Division – no disrespect to them but they weren't good enough. At the end of the season, if your contract ran out, the club offered you the minimum wage of £7 per week. If you declined the only place you could go was into non-league which is what happened to Michael Barnard. Mike made enquiries and found out that you had to inform the Football League and the Football Association who you were keeping and who was being offered a new contract. Cox failed to inform the FA (not the Football League), who ran non-league football, so he lost all the transfer money. I would also have gone out of the league but for Reading coming in.

Norman would have made a good scout. He told me when I first arrived he didn't think I'd make it, as I was a bit slow to turn as a full-back. I put in a lot of work in training with Peter Harris, who had blistering pace, which worked for me, so I listened to what he said. It was a shrewd assessment.

John Phillips

Norman had always been a bit of a clown, the mad Irishman. He wasn't the tallest of keepers but was extremely brave and was always a cad in the dressing room. One of his favourite things at training was when we were running round the track at Fratton Park and all of a sudden over the tannoy out comes the voice, 'Does your head keep slipping off the pillow at night? If so use Fuzzo the wonder hair restorer.' Of course it was Norman and if you were thinning in those days they would take the mick out of people.

When Freddie Cox took over he was a terrible man, he ruined Pompey and they didn't recover for years. The local press gave him stick so he banned all the players from giving interviews to the paper. Norman ignored it and gave an interview, so Cox made him train on his own – a full international – dreadful. Derek Dougan left, as did Ray Crawford, Johnny Gordon, Mick Barnard, Tom McGhee, Bill Albury and myself and he brought in Third Division players. It was little wonder Pompey finished bottom of the Second Division and the club was in the doldrums for years. I could never understand why they didn't get rid of him earlier. He didn't like characters and that was his downfall; he was ok with schoolboys and 'yes' men, but with experienced pros he didn't have a clue. We weren't allowed to go drinking after Tuesday. Cox would get the trainers to come round the houses and check on different players to make sure they were indoors by 10.30 p.m. Norman lived in a Victorian house he rented from the club and his garden backed on to Fratton Park. He would go down the bottom of his garden, jump over the wall into the ground and sneak out without anyone seeing him. Of course he used to come back that way.

Jimmy Stephen

Norman was a one-off character, full of fun. When we played away from home, it was normal for the goalkeeper, right back and left back to room together, so he a was a room-mate of mine on many occasions. He was a brilliant goalkeeper, very brave and consistent, and what I remember most is his injury against Sheffield Wednesday. A ball went through and Norman caught it; he had his hands round it on the deck and Derek Dooley should have jumped over him. Instead he put his big size ten boot right into Norman's hand, which was a dreadful, unnecessary thing to do. The referee can't have seen what happened, but I did as I was following behind Dooley.

RAMSGATE FC

Phil Winfield

I was captain when Norman played – I came down in 1959 from Lincoln City and played at Ramsgate for about six years. Just from Norman's name it was a big signing for us. He wasn't the goalkeeper he had been, but it did create interest at Ramsgate. We only saw him Saturday afternoons; he didn't train with us, so we really didn't get to know him that well. He drifted in about an hour before kick-off and went straight after the game. Every time Norman caught a ball awkwardly his fingers would dislocate. He would pull them out and get on with the game!

Vince Thomas

I think Norman played for less than a season at Ramsgate, leaving about two-thirds of the way through. He was popular with the crowd and always well received. In Norman's day the average gate was about 2000, but we went bust in the late 1970s and almost folded, but were back in the Rymans League by 2005. It was a long time coming and we lost a lot of support, but there are still many supporters like me who go back a long way and will remember Norman. He wore strapping on his right hand, which must have dated back to the Dooley incident.

You could see, even at that stage of his career, he had been a great goalie. His best display was in the autumn against Sittingbourne, who were top of Division One of the Southern League. Someone tried to get Norman to throw that game as well, but he was outstanding on the day in a goalless draw. The Northern Ireland selectors actually watched him in a match at Corby. In one game he played at Margate it was so cold Norman put his hands in hot water at half-time. There is a nice connection with Walter Rickett, who played for Blackpool in the 1948 FA Cup Final. As a boy Norman watched him play. Walter then signed him for Ramsgate all those years later as manager.

NORTHERN IRELAND

Billy Bingham

During my time, Norman deputised for Harry Gregg, the up-and-coming goalkeeper, for a few games. He was an excellent goalkeeper the whole time I was with him in the Irish team. He had very good hands and great distribution of the ball too. When an attack was broken up and he got hold of the ball, he distributed it well. Norman had a nonchalant way in terms of passing things off and he was so funny off the park, full of wisecracks. Gerry Morgan and he always had a good repartee with each other. Gerry was always full of cracks to cheer everybody up and take the pressure off before big games, and Norman was the same. Some people thought it was a bit over the top in terms of being light-hearted, but it was one way of easing the pressure of being the goalkeeper. He was a character that people didn't take too seriously off the park, but he was very funny with a good sense of humour.

Jimmy McIlroy

Norman was a superb goalkeeper; some of his saves were amazing, diving at the feet of centre-forwards renowned for thumping goalkeepers. I can understand why he had so many injuries – it was because he was a top-class, fearless keeper. You need to be a bit daft to be a good keeper; some people might say as he was Irish, he was so thick he didn't know what he was doing. It took someone like

Harry Gregg, who was rated number one goalkeeper in the world, to take his place.

There was always tremendous banter between Norman and Gerry Morgan as they were both great characters and got on like a house on fire. I don't think Gerry was endowed with a lot of medical knowledge – he was a traditional, bucket and sponge man, but he was a great old boy for keeping everybody's spirits high in the dressing room. As we were ready to go onto the field Gerry would say, 'Come on lads, pull yourselves to pieces.' He would talk about Preston Both Ends or Manchester Divided!

Getting to the World Cup finals in 1958 was virtually a miracle. We were barely a dot on the footballing world before then. After the match we lost against Argentina, we were back at the hotel singing as if we had won. It was almost as if we couldn't take it seriously and it was all a big joke. Our attitude was that we never dreamt in a million years we would ever get to the World Cup finals. We played five games in thirteen days, travelled all over the country in the coach and in the final game against France were drawing 0 – 0 at half-time but then ran out of steam. I was lucky enough to play with top players in both the Irish and Burnley teams. There was more joking and acting the 'goat' when the Irish lads got together than any other international team in the world. Norman was a very important member of the Irish team, not only for his play but also his personality.

We were playing Portsmouth at Turf Moor and Norman and I had been selected to play for the Irish team the following Saturday at Belfast. The Portsmouth team travelled by train to Preston and there was a bus waiting for them to be driven to Turf Moor. After the match Norman got on the bus back to Preston, then on a busy road thumbed a lift on a coal lorry which went all the way to Lancaster, which is close to Heysham. He then made his way to the quayside, where you could buy a penny ticket out of a machine, so you could walk to where the steamer was anchored. Norman waited until a woman came along with a case and a baby in a pram. He apparently said, 'Let me help you,' picked up the pram and walked up the gangplank. There was always someone at the end of the gangplank waiting to check your ticket, so Norman put his penny ticket in his mouth and the fella waved him on and he found a big chair to doze through the night. Only Norman could have travel from Burnley to Belfast for a penny!

I've always had a soft spot for Norman. Life hadn't been easy for him but he always put on a brave face and was a very likeable person. He was very much the life and soul of the party; I can never remember him being anything other than cheerful. He talked what I would call cockney slang, with an Irish accent. The last time I saw him was at a dinner at Hillsborough Castle. He was wearing more jewellery than I owned – more and more rings!

Peter McParland

I remember Norman way back in about 1946 when he was playing for Distillery Seconds in the Intermediate League. The name stuck with me as a thirteen year-old watching him as they played my home town team Newry Town in a league game.

One of the early games I played with Norman for Northern Ireland was in 1955 against Scotland at Windsor Park. Scotland had a fair team, but we got at them and got our noses in front, and Norman played a big part in that victory. I remember the Czechoslovakia play-off game in Sweden, when Norman injured his hand, was a great display on the day. I have seen a photo after the game with us all celebrating on the pitch, and Norman is showing the Czech forward where he kicked his hand. The lad had come over to congratulate him and Norman showed, in a friendly way, his injured hand. The next day Norman had his hand tied up and was limping along as we left for the quarter-final. By the time we played France we were very tired, having to travel by train over 250 miles. Playing the next day, it was not the best way to get ready for the quarter-final of the World Cup, especially as the French team had been able to rest up.

You could shoulder charge in those days and even though Norman was an international teammate of mine, when I played for Aston Villa against him, he wasn't immune from that as far as I was concerned. I didn't show any mercy playing against him and remember giving him a shoulder charge over the line. He was shouting at me to cut it out, but it wasn't my way to hold back. When I first played against Pompey they were a bit of a handful with Jimmy Dickinson, Jack Froggatt and Harris and Henderson on the wings, an excellent team but they faded in the late 1950s.

All round Norman was a fine goalkeeper in an age when they weren't always tall like now. He was courageous, didn't shirk anything, he attacked balls in the goalmouth and got them, and his reactions were good at getting down to balls. He had all the cockney rhyming slang amongst the players all the time and was full of life. Harry Gregg and I kept in touch with Norman; he was a smashing lad who enjoyed life and I was very sad when he passed away.

Morton McKnight

I've known Norman for about thirty years. He came back to Ireland in the late 1960s when I was secretary of Distillery Football Club, who sold Norman to Arsenal, and we had many jars of beer together. I became president of the Irish Football League until the League merged with the Association and I was made vice-president of the Association, a role I held until June 2010. I am now an honorary life member. During my spell there I saw it as my role to make sure the surviving members of the 1958 squad weren't forgotten. I first brought them over in 2005 for the international against Germany and put them up for a few days, then in 2008 against the Czech Republic. I managed to get them over again just before Christmas 2010 for the Italy game, but Norman couldn't make it as he was taken into hospital. Perhaps I'm a bit of a romantic as all those guys were my idols at the time, and known for their modesty, but I tried to do my bit.

Maurice Magee

Norman was ten years older than me to the day and I knew him as I also lived in Wellington Street. The part Norman lived in was affectionately known as 'The Belgian Row', as they were built to house Belgian refugees during the First World War, though none ever lived in them. Norman lived at 34 Wellington Street, the third house. It was very much a mixed area, but people got on well together. A lot of the streets in Lurgan were predominantly Catholic or Protestant and, as in a mixed community, they had their differences, but shared their differences. There was no organised junior football in the area at the time and Norman had quite a few friends who were attached to St Peter's Club, which was only formed in the early 1940s. His friends played Gaelic football, so he joined in and played with them. Bobby Carville was a character and a founder member of St Peter's. His barber shop was a meeting place about three doors from where I lived. A ten minute haircut would take an hour, as there were always arguments. Bobby would get his reference book out and point his razor at somebody to prove his point.

In the 1940s, there was nothing else for kids to do other than play sport. I remember Norman playing football in our street with about forty others; they played diagonally across the road with a telephone pole on one side and the house on the other as the goals, so it was only about six foot wide. Another pole was outside Bobby's shop and we played with a tennis ball. Although he was a goalkeeper I remember when he came back from Arsenal one summer, he headed the tennis ball against the wall a hundred times, so he had that skill as well.

I am a past secretary of St Peter's and was also the leader in charge of the youth club for eight years, and captain of the minor and senior teams. It was a wonderful evening when Norman finally received his medal in 2004. Amongst the people there was Maurice O'Reilly. Maurice and Norman were great buddies – he played for St Peter's and also won an Ireland championship medal at minor level for Armagh Minors in 1949. Paul McGrane, one of the guests of honour, was captain of the Armagh county team at the time and one of the best midfielders Armagh has ever produced. Josie McDonald was one of the boys who met Norman in Bobby Carville's shop and followed his career closely. His father Tom helped to train the minor team Norman played in.

Lurgan was Norman's real home, we're very friendly people here and whenever he visited he never wanted to go back.

Malcolm Brodie

Norman was technically superb, fearless, exceptionally good at timing dives and cutting out crosses, and also a talker. He could drive on the back four, as you would call it today, in front of him and the banter between him and the full backs Dick Keith and Alfie McMichael was quite something else. It helped him to create the confidence of the defence, which was first class as they had a great understanding, inspired overall by Peter Doherty, a superb manager and by Danny Blanchflower.

Norman and I were the only survivors of the tour of Canada and USA in 1953. It was a coast-to-coast tour organised by Sam Donaghy in conjunction with the Canadian Football Association. We left Belfast to Liverpool on the *Empress of Scotland*. The first game was in New York where we played Liverpool, including Billy Liddell and Bob Paisley, before moving out to the west coast of America. We left New York on a Saturday night for Hamilton and Ontario in a sleeper train. What impressed the players most was when the Sunday newspapers came in early and for the first time in their life the team realised that the Sunday papers in the States were like a book compared to what they had back home. They carried them onto the train and were astounded by it. It was the first indication they were living in a different world. You have to remember, it came soon after the end of the Second World War. The team played a remarkable game in Sasketchewan. It was originally scheduled on a park pitch but the rain came down and created a complete mud surface. If you stepped onto it you could hardly get your boots out, so overnight they switched to another pitch. The two teams got changed at the only hotel in Moose Jaw and the Canadian side, which included a lot of Polish immigrants, virtually changed their line-up at half-time. During the match a dog came onto the pitch and wherever the ball went the dog went too and it became a total farce. There were four goals from Eddie McMorran, two from Tommy Casey, two from Bruce Shiels and the others from Jimmy D'Arcy and Norman Lockhart. The other high scoring match was at Edmonton when we won 9 – 1 – Sammy Hughes scored four, McMorran three and Eddie Crossan two. The final game we were beaten 4 – 1 by the Berne Young

Boys of Switzerland. People thought we were going to play against a schoolboy team, but it was the name of a professional outfit in Switzerland. Norman was one of the life and souls of the party on that particular trip; he was the guy who had his own individual type of fun and banter.

The other joker in the pack was Gerry Morgan, another great character, known as Uncle Gerry, the guy who made the family spirit and the expert on one-liners. He looked after the players – every morning at about 7 a.m. he was knocking on everyone's door with a can of Andrews Liver Salts and each player had a spoonful. This became a tradition, not only on that tour but also in the 1958 World Cup. We set up at Tylosand and when we arrived, there was this young Swedish twelve-year-old boy called Bengt Jonasson, who came round the camp. Gerry and Norman took a shine to him; he would run messages for them and was soon adopted as mascot to the team. He could speak perfect English and travelled round the country with us. When we left Sweden Danny Blanchflower said we should do something for him, as he was in tears as we left Norrkoping for Stockholm. We decided to bring him over to Belfast in the October for the next international against England and gave him a VIP welcome. He has retained this friendship with the Irish FA and since then has become a leading businessman in Stockholm.

The squad came home by air from Stockholm. In order to avoid all the publicity Harry Gregg decided he would leave twenty four hours earlier, which was very fortunate. I went to see the team off as I was staying behind to report on the rest of the Finals and as the plane got into the air the undercarriage wouldn't retract and they had to circle the airport for an hour to use up the fuel before making an emergency landing. It was a blessing in disguise that Harry wasn't on that flight; it would have been a horrific experience for him so soon after Munich.

Of all the Northern Ireland international teams I have covered over the years, that 1958 squad was the one that had the special bonding. For the first time in international football they had made an impact. They went to Sweden with the smallest side numerically, were decimated by injury, yet reached the quarter finals. Every one of them was part of an experiment, a new era for Northern Ireland, but whenever their careers finished they retained that friendship and bond.

Ted Hinton, Bill Smyth and Tommy Breen were the Irish keepers before Norman came onto the scene. His transfer to English football thrust him into the top bracket and he became a pin-up boy. In addition to the Scotland (1955) and Spain (1958) matches, Norman had an outstanding series in Sweden. He played exceptionally well even though he was injured. We had terrible trouble with goalkeeping injury problems but he was fantastic there. As a keeper, Norman was always under the shadow of Harry, but nonetheless proved an outstanding professional both in the Irish League and in England and internationals.

As a person, Norman was a wonderful Irish loveable rogue, the artful dodger who never got into trouble, one of the gloriously irreverent characters of the 1950s. Life to him meant celebrating and he enjoyed every minute of it. Every day was Christmas Day or St Patrick's.